Wenceslaus Hollar

Wenceslaus Hollar

A Bohemian Artist in England

Richard T. Godfrey

Yale Center for British Art

Yale University Press
New Haven and London

This book is published in conjunction with an exhibition at the Yale Center for British Art, New Haven, Connecticut, 16 November 1994 through 22 January 1995.

Frontispiece: *A Group of Muffs*, etching, 1647. Collection of N.G. Stogdon.

Designed by Lisa C. Tremaine
Set in Minion type by Highwood Typographic Services, Hamden, Connecticut
Printed in the United States of America by
Thomson-Shore, Inc., Dexter, Michigan,
and Hull Printing Company, Inc.,
Meriden, Connecticut

Library of Congress Cataloging-in-Publication Data
Hollar, Wenceslaus, 1607–1677.
Wenceslaus Hollar: a Bohemian artist in England /Richard T. Godfrey.
p. cm.
Catalog of an exhibition held at the Yale Center for British Art,
November 16, 1994–January 22, 1995.
Includes bibliographical references (p.   ) and index.
ISBN 0-300-06166-8 (cloth: alk. paper)
ISBN 0-930606-74-4 (paper: alk. paper)
1. Hollar, Wenceslaus, 1607–1677—Exhibitions. I. Godfrey, Richard T.
II. Yale Center for British Art. III. Title.
N6797.H65A4   1994
760'.092—dc20   94-21730
                                                                  CIP

A catalogue record for this book is available from the British Library.

The paper in this book meets the guidelines for permanence and durability of the Committee on Production Guidelines for Book Longevity of the Council on Library Resources.

10 9 8 7 6 5 4 3 2 1

Contents

Foreword

The career of Wenceslaus Hollar reflected, as it spanned, one of the most turbulent periods of British history. Invited to England by the courtier and collector Thomas Howard, Earl of Arundel, he lived to see the aristocratic culture of Caroline England first leveled by the Civil War and then partially restored. Artists were not immune to such fundamental social changes, as the courts and households to which they had been attached were dissolved and they were thrown into the precarious independence of the open marketplace. Hollar was one of the first to make that transition, however involuntarily, and, by means of sheer productivity, to survive as a self-employed artist. The range of his work is extraordinary: war and peace, town and country; fur, fish, flesh, and fowl—all rendered with a precision which matched his almost obsessive eye for detail. In Restoration London, he explored virtually every avenue open to the commercial engraver. Visually, he was an encyclopedist, decades before the eighteenth century invented the term.

To Richard Godfrey, print specialist and scholar, we are especially indebted for this exhibition and catalogue. He returns to the Center as guest curator for the third time and is warmly welcomed. To peerless knowledge of the field he adds both enthusiasm and a refreshing originality of thought. At the Center it was Patrick Noon, curator of prints, drawings, and rare books, who encouraged Godfrey's proposal and brought it to pass; he joins me in expressing thanks to the lenders who have enabled us to realize the first comprehensive and monographic exhibition in North America devoted to Wenceslaus Hollar.

We also would like to thank Judy Metro and Yale University Press for publishing this catalogue. Finally, we record a compound debt of gratitude to Suzanne Beebe, Richard Caspole, Susan Casteras, Constance Clement, Theresa Fairbanks, Richard Field, Ralph Franklin, Vincent Giroud, Timothy Goodhue, Ferenc Gyorgyey, Lisa Hodermarsky, Marilyn Hunt, Julie Lavorgna, Mary Mayer, Heidi Myers, Jules Prown, Kim Rannala, Elizabeth Valeika, Lorie Watson, and Martha Yellig, all colleagues in New Haven who have contributed to the success of this venture.

Duncan Robinson
Director

Acknowledgments

Wenceslaus Hollar is not, nor ever was, a neglected artist. He was well known and respected in his own time (though ill remunerated), and the value of his work immediately recognized by such informed contemporaries as John Evelyn and John Aubrey. He was keenly collected in the eighteenth century, and, from his many interests, George Vertue selected Hollar as a special subject. His rarest prints were high performers at auctions; the set of *Shells,* which belonged to John Barnard, foremost among English print collectors, sold for £20 in 1798 at the auction house of Thomas Philipe. In the same sale Barnard's five impressions from the five states of Rembrandt's etching *The Three Crosses,* and his five impressions of three states of *Christ Presented to the People,* fetched the combined sum of £23.18.0. This enthusiasm was maintained in the nineteenth century, and Sir Francis Seymour-Haden—surgeon, etcher, and grand panjandrum of print pundits—waxed lyrical on the subject of Hollar's technique.

In the twentieth century Hollar's work has frequently been the subject of exhibitions, most notably in London, Manchester, Prague, Paris, and Berlin. But there had not been an exhibition in the United States that presented the full range of Hollar's work, drawings as well as prints, and this venture is intended to redress the imbalance.

The scope of Hollar's work is almost boundless—from portraits to fur muffs to architecture—and its value to historians is obvious. He was a son of Prague, and he is still much valued there, though in a lecture given in that city I was somewhat surprised to find my audience blissfully unaware of the artist's London years. But it is the English, and Londoners in particular, who are most greatly in his debt for his record of the city before it was devastated by fire.

This exhibition is not primarily concerned with Hollar's role as a documenter of his times, but rather with his virtues (and sometimes his limitations) as an artist and with the beauty of his technique. The first guideline for the selection of most exhibits has been aesthetic, not antiquarian. If there were to be a subtitle it would be "Hollar and His Lines," not "Hollar and His Times." In the end, of course, it ended up being both.

In most exhibitions the curator drags with him to the finish line a large bundle of obligation and indebtedness, not least to friends and colleagues to whose ears the very sound of the artist's name has become wearisome. I record my thanks to Catherine Bindman, Jana Brabcová, Thomas Buhler, Andrew Clary, Cara Denison, Diana Dethloff, Judy Egerton, George R. Goldner, George Gordon, Antony Griffiths, Ben Johnson, Susan Kaye, Susan Lambert, Paul McCarron, Dr. Nicholas Penny, Charles E. Pierce, Jr., the Hon. Jane Roberts, Susan Schulman, Gillian Singer, Lindsay Stainton, Marika Thompson, Dustin Wees, Dr. Christopher White, and Hilary Williams. I am most grateful to Craig Hartley for reading a draft of the essay.

Peter Freeth, master etcher and admirer of Hollar, kindly spent a day reminding me of some of the basic principles of etching.

I am particularly grateful to my colleague Belinda Hargreave for help in many ways, not least in the management of a laptop computer and for somehow tolerating the creeping weekend invasion of our office by large chunks of my personal library.

The project has been blessed by particularly helpful private lenders who have followed its vicissitudes with as much concern as they would show had they been the artist's family and friends. In the United States I am particularly grateful to Dr. Howard Fox and Frank Raysor II, who have both lent most generously. In addition, their careful inventories of their collections have been most helpful.

I am grateful to the Trustees of the Chatsworth Settlement for their most generous loans. Peter Day, Keeper of Collections at Chatsworth, has been helpful in every respect.

In England Robert Harding has not only lent many prints from his Hollar-Arundel collection, but he conjured up—seemingly with a snap of his fingers—the long-lost inventory of the deceased Hollar's household goods. This list, reproduced with the kind permission of the dean and chapter of Westminster Abbey, is the single most important contribution to the exhibition. Samuel Josefowitz not only lent his beautiful set of the *German Views,* but he also cut the mounts with a craftsmanship well suited to the contents. Christopher Mendez is not only a lender but a long-standing admirer of Hollar. It was he who spotted Hollar's touching last *View of Prague,* which was unremarked in a hurriedly catalogued bundle of Hollar prints at Sotheby's, London, in June 1989. The blushing cataloguer (myself) now pays penance by sending this rare print on its way to the Friends of the National Gallery at Prague.

At a crucial moment Nicholas Stogdon and Carol Bundy Stogdon gave me hospitality in Somerset, and they have been a continuous source of strength, despite being sorely tried. I appreciate Nicholas Stogdon's attempts to teach a singularly inept pupil the mysteries of inserting Czech accents into the text, though at the time my appreciation was expressed somewhat tersely.

My greatest personal debt is to Caroline Elam, who has always encouraged me and listened with equal patience to the manifold lamentations and exultations of a Hollar enthusiast. It was also her erudition that informed me of the whereabouts of the original drawing of the so-called *Pagan Sacrifice* after "Mantegna."

This is the third exhibition at the Yale Center for British Art with which I have been associated, and I am thankful for the Center's continuing hospitality. Patrick Noon has endured with his usual sangfroid not merely a host of tiresome phone calls, letters, and faxes, but a manuscript that was not so much delivered as strewn from afar in a series of disconnected episodes. I am also grateful to Patrick and to Diane Tsurutani for their friendship and hospitality over the past fifteen years. Any visitor to the Yale Center for British Art, let alone a guest curator, must pay homage to Paul Mellon, whose creation it is. My first contact with his collection of British art was in the winter of 1964 when it was shown in London at the Royal Academy. I remember the occasion for a forceful argument with a fellow art student as to the merits of George Stubbs's painting of a zebra. Was it art, or was it zoological illustration? I won (it is art), and the occasion kindled an interest in the then little suspected variety of British art. Since 1979 one of the most enjoyable benedictions of my career has been my association with the Yale Center for British Art. To its director, Duncan Robinson, and to all its staff, past and present, I offer my thanks.

The subject of this exhibition seems to have had scant regard for his parents, not forgiving his father's attempts to obstruct his career. I am afflicted by no such inhibitions, and here I proffer my heartfelt gratitude to my mother, Mary, for kindnesses too numerous to list. My father, the Reverend John Godfrey, F.S.A., a clergyman-scholar in the old tradition of the Church of England, died when his retirement had scarcely begun. He would have appreciated Hollar, and it is to my father's memory that this work is dedicated.

Lenders to the Exhibition

Beinecke Rare Book and Manuscript Library,
  Yale University

British Museum, London

Duke of Devonshire and the Trustees of the
  Chatsworth Settlement

Dr. and Mrs. Howard A. Fox

Richard T. Godfrey

Robert J. D. Harding

Josefowitz Collection

Medical Library, Yale University

Christopher Mendez

Metropolitan Museum of Art, New York

Pierpont Morgan Library, New York

Frank W. Raysor II

N. G. Stogdon

Victoria and Albert Museum, London

Yale Center for British Art

Yale University Art Gallery

Private collections

Hollar Chronology

1607 Born in Prague on 23 July to a Protestant family.

1612 Death of the Emperor Rudolf II.

1620 Battle of the White Mountain outside Prague and defeat of the Protestant Bohemian Estates. Frederick V of Bohemia flees the country.

1625 First dated etching.

1627 Edict of Ferdinand II on 31 July ordering members of the Bohemian nobility to convert to Catholicism within six months or to emigrate. Hollar leaves Bohemia at some point in this year.

1627–1628 Active in Stuttgart.

1629–1630 Active in Strasbourg, employed by the publisher Jacob van der Heyden.

1631–1632 Active in Frankfurt, working for the publisher and engraver Matthaeus Merian.

1634 Travels to Holland, makes drawings in Amsterdam and other cities.

1634–1636 Active in Cologne. Makes a number of journeys up the Rhine.

1636 The Earl of Arundel and his embassy pass through Cologne; Hollar enters the service of the earl and travels with him to Regensburg, Vienna, and Prague, arriving in London at the end of December.

c. 1640 Acts as *serviteur domestique* to the Duke of York.

1641 Marries Mistress Tracey, a lady-in-waiting to the Countess of Arundel; she dies in 1652.

1642 Beginning of the English Civil War. The court is established at Oxford. London is a Parliamentarian stronghold. The Earl of Arundel leaves for Antwerp, later traveling to Padua.

1644 At some stage in this year he travels to Antwerp. According to an old legend Hollar was captured at the siege of Basing House in 1645 with Inigo Jones. This seems impossible—and fortunate for Hollar, since most of the garrison was put to the sword by Cromwell's troops.

1644–1652 Active in Antwerp, working for a variety of publishers.

1649 Execution of Charles I.

1651 End of the Civil War.

1652 Hollar returns to London.

1653 Oliver Cromwell becomes Lord Protector of the Commonwealth.

1656 Marries a woman named Honora, who is to outlive him.

1660 Return of Charles II and the restoration of the monarchy.

1665 His son dies in the plague.

1666 Appointed King's Scenographer to Charles II. The Great Fire destroys much of London.

1669 Travels to the colony of Tangier as official draftsman.

1677 Dies on 25 March and is buried in St. Margaret's, Westminster.

Wenceslaus Hollar

The art of Wenceslaus Hollar is, first of all, about lines. Curved lines to track the gentle contours of a hill, ruled lines to indicate an overcast sky, modulated border lines to enclose the design artfully. Hollar was an artist constant in his affections, loyal to his roots, and devoted to a repertoire of forms and lines that is simple but individual and sometimes poetic. The lines of few other artists have been devoted to such a multiplicity of experiences, travels, and subjects.

Hollar, who was brought up in Prague, learned his craft in Germany but profited most from his study of Dutch landscape prints of the Haarlem school. The vital core of his work is to be found in his English years, yet many of his finest plates were etched in Antwerp. His very name had, chameleonlike, adapted to his changes of residence; he was Václav Hollar in his native Bohemia, Wenzel in Germany, Wenceslaus in England. In 1661, wary of his creditors, he even adopted a French persona, directing John Aubrey that "if you had occasion to ask for mee of the people of the house, then you must say the Frenchman Limner for they know not my name perfectly, for reasons sake otherwise you may go up directly."[1]

Yet Hollar was never in doubt about his nationality; he was born a Bohemian, and he died a Bohemian. He expired in harness to the London publishers, wearily engaged in the drudgery of illustrating Thoroton's *Antiquities of Nottinghamshire,* but his last significant print is a small view of Prague drawn and etched with extreme refinement (no. 127). Signed and dated 1676, the year before he died, it brings Hollar's career full circle. The print, with "Zu Prag" neatly lettered in the sky, is of a view across the River Vltava; in the distance are Hradčany Castle and the fortifications of St. Lorenzberg. For Hollar, aged sixty-nine and eking out a bare sustenance in a London rising from the ashes of the Great Fire, this little plate was an exercise in nostalgia. Only two impressions are known, and such a modest and remote subject, devoid of

architectural interest, could have had scant commercial purpose. In fact, the artist had turned to his stock in trade, his sketchbooks, to unearth a drawing now lost but from the same period—perhaps the same day—as a related drawing in the John Rylands Library sketchbook, showing the same view from a slightly different angle, and dated 1626.[2] Hollar still was thinking of his native city, which he had last seen in 1636, and it is evident that the river and the great mass of the hill beyond it were of special significance to him.[3]

Hollar was born in Prague on 23 July 1607, the son of Jan Hollar, a register of the law court at Prague who was knighted by Rudolf II, and Margaret, who was also a member of the minor nobility.[4] Throughout his life the matter of his social rank was of considerable importance to the artist. The nature of his religious faith has been much debated, but both John Aubrey and John Evelyn, who knew the artist well, are unequivocal on the subject. Aubrey states that Hollar's father was a "knight of the Empire and a Protestant, and either for keeping a conventicle, or being taken at one, forfeited his Estate, and was ruined by the Roman Catholiques." He further notes that "Wincislaus dyed a Catholique," and John Evelyn writes that Hollar was "perverted at last by the Jesuits at Antwerp to change his religion."[5] Recent research has confirmed these statements, and it has been demonstrated that Hollar's family worshiped with the evangelical Bohemian Brethren.[6] In Hollar's art, however, religious fervor is noted only by its absence.

The Prague in which Hollar was born was the city of Rudolf II, Holy Roman Emperor, whose consuming passion for the arts had attracted to his court an army of artists and craftsmen in addition to scientists, astronomers, and natural philosophers (fig. 1). Rudolfine art, especially in its figurative mode, occupies the farthest and most convoluted branches of international court mannerism.[7] *Moderation* was a word deleted from its vocabulary. The paintings of Bartolommeus

Spranger, who worked at Rudolf's court from 1580 until his death in 1611, show the school at its most erotic and sophisticated. Serpentine naked goddesses, polished and lathered, intertwine with their celestial partners in postures of boneless contraposto. His designs, and those of Hans von Aachen and Joseph Heintz, were given wide European circulation through engravings by artists of the Haarlem school, notably Hendrick Goltzius, whose dazzling engraved lines match the virtuosity of the originals.[8] For sculpture Rudolf had access to Adrian de Vries, whose bronze figures, poised in space, are matched only by those of Giovanni da Bologna—an artist Rudolf was unable to entice to Prague.[9] Landscapes were represented by the entangled alpine scenes of Roelandt Savery, who also excelled in still life. The works that Hollar perhaps found most sympathetic were the illuminations and manuscripts of Georg Hoefnagel, which combine naturalism with allegory.[10]

A rise in the stature of the artist's profession was a natural by-product of this renaissance. Artists were well paid and recognized in society, and Von Aachen even became an intimate of the emperor. Rudolf himself painted and constantly patrolled the studios, watching the artists work and proffering his advice. Engravers were not excluded from this royal bene-

diction, and the foremost engraver in Prague, Aegidius Sadeler, was summoned from Flanders to Prague in 1597 and appointed to the specially created post of imperial printmaker (Kupferstecher). He was a versatile engraver, capable of emulating the swelling and tapering lines of Goltzius in prints after Spranger, but he was also able to adopt a lighter and more prosaic manner. He was a prolific engraver of landscape, copying the work of the imperial painters Paul Brill, Pieter Stephens, and Roelandt Savery. These prints, characterized by agitated foliage, dense forests, and terrifying vistas, must have been very familiar to Hollar, but they seem to have left no lasting imprint on his own feeling for landscape. Sadeler remained in Prague until his death in 1629, thus the youthful Hollar would have had ample opportunity to visit his studio, and Sadeler, or a member of his school, might well have been Hollar's first instructor in the art of printmaking.[11]

It is impossible to know what first-hand knowledge Hollar might have had of Rudolf's collection, much of which was preserved in cabinets and displayed only for the benefit of the privileged. He might, however, have seen some of the more accessible art in the palace, where his father worked, and such public images as the frescoes on the facade of Spranger's house. Prints he could see in abundance, judging from Sadeler's large 1607 engraving *The Vladislav Hall in the Hradčany Castle, Prague* (no. 1). A fair is in progress, and prominently displayed at the left is a print seller's stall. Prints hang in serried ranks, fluttering in the breeze from the great window behind, and the print seller and his assistant fetch bundles of prints for an absorbed collector. Such displays must have included prints by Sadeler and members of his school, and they no doubt also featured the Dutch and Flemish prints that so influenced Hollar. It is also probable that they featured maps, perhaps including the large world maps published by Claesz Janz Visscher in Amsterdam, their borders enlivened by representations of the inhabitants of the different countries in their characteristic garb.[12]

John Aubrey records that when Hollar was a "schoole-boy he tooke a delight in draweing of mapps; which draughts he kept, and they were pretty . . . so that what he did for his delight and recreation only when a boy, proved to be his live-lyhood when a man."[13] Our knowledge of Hollar's beginnings as an etcher—probably as an interested young amateur rather than a fledgling professional—has been enlarged by Craig Hartley's discovery of a cache of juvenile prints in the Fitz-william Museum.[14] Nervously scratched on little scraps of left-

1. Aegidius Sadeler, *Emperor Rudolf II*. Engraving. Metropolitan Museum of Art, New York.

A

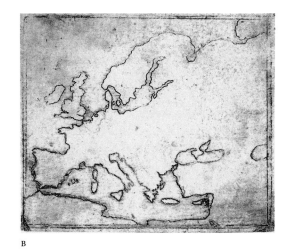

B

C

D

2A. Wenceslaus Hollar. *Mars and Venus Netted by Vulcan.* Etching. Fitzwilliam Museum, Cambridge.

2B. Wenceslaus Hollar. *Map of Europe.* Etching. Fitzwilliam Museum, Cambridge.

2C. Wenceslaus Hollar. *Two Views of Prague.* Etching. Fitzwilliam Museum, Cambridge.

2D. Wenceslaus Hollar. *Frederick V of Bohemia.* Etching. Fitzwilliam Museum, Cambridge.

over copper, the etchings fall into distinct groups: copies and adaptations of Dürer and the German little masters, such as Hans Sebald Beham; landscapes in the manner of Sadeler; and portraits of Frederick V of Bohemia. They also include a deftly sketched *Mars and Venus Netted by Vulcan* (a markedly Rudolfine subject), an outline map of Europe, and two views of Prague (figs. 2A–2D). In these early efforts Hollar is trying, with limited success, to master the difficulties posed by the plate's first exposure to the acid. They are hesitantly executed,

snatched too quickly from the acid, but their subjects are revealing. Many artists must have begun thus and discarded the results; it is typical of Hollar to have kept them, like the maps that Aubrey saw. This preservation of his work was evidently archival in spirit.

Dürer had been a great favorite at the Prague court, and to etch adaptations of his work was entirely in the Rudolfine spirit. The portraits of Frederick V, copied from a 1622 engraving by Willem Delff after Mierevelt, have another significance,

3

for they surely reveal sympathy with that unhappy monarch. Frederick was chosen king in 1619 by the Protestant assembly at Prague. His consort was Queen Elizabeth, the daughter of James I, and thus the sister of the future Charles I. They had fled Bohemia after Frederick's army suffered catastrophic defeat by imperial forces at the Battle of the White Mountain in 1620. But the disintegration of the tolerant Bohemian culture had already begun. Rudolf died in 1612, and his successor, the Emperor Matthias, moved the Imperial Court to Vienna. Wagonloads of Rudolf's collections followed him, artists' salaries were reduced, and the artists themselves began to leave Prague. The youthful Hollar must have been aware that the future for aspiring artists was bleak.

Hollar took the first steps in his peripatetic career in 1627, when he left Prague. He was only twenty, but it is likely that the move had been on his mind for some time, partly because of his father's opposition to his artistic ambitions. This is emphasized in the brief biography, obviously authorized by Hollar, that accompanies the portrait of him by Jan Meyssens that was etched by Hollar and published in Antwerp in 1649 (no. 75). The biography notes that Hollar was a "gentilhomme ne a Prage l'an 1607, a este de nature fort inclin pour l'art de meniature principalement pour esclaircir, mais beaucoup retarde par son pere, l'an 1627, il est party de Prage, aijant demeure en divers lieux en Allemagne." The increasing discrimination against Protestants must have been further impetus for the move. After the Battle of the White Mountain, Catholicism was imposed on the mainly Protestant population, and in 1627 the ancient Bohemian constitution was abolished by the Emperor Ferdinand. With the Thirty Years War in its bloody infancy, Hollar must have given careful consideration to his destination.

The pen drawing *Fortune* (no. 2), dated 1625 by a later hand, is one of Hollar's earliest surviving drawings. In it Fortuna is perched on a globe above a raging sea that threatens to overwhelm a number of wallowing galleons. Lightning divides the sky, and Fortuna's garment transforms itself into a billowing sail. It is almost certain that Hollar had never seen the sea, and his vision of a distant harbor and his schematically rendered waves owe much to Flemish prints of the previous century. Hollar copied Aldegrever's little print of Fortune in 1626, but the serpentine pose of the figure in *Fortune* owes more to mannerist sources.[15] It is an immature and derivative work but drawn with vivacity, and the subject may have greater significance than previously realized. It is evidently intended as a

metaphor for the perils of travel, and it is tempting to link it with the artist's own departure from Prague into an unmapped future. It should perhaps be associated with a drawing now at Dessau, signed and dated "1st January 1628," inscribed "made in Stuttgart," and sketched for one of the *Album Amicorum* (Friendship Albums) then popular in Germany, to which the owner's friends contributed drawings, poems, or personal inscriptions. It features a partly clad man clutching the caduceus of Mercury (but without Mercury's other attributes) and jumping onto dry land. Behind him a ship founders in heavy seas. A Latin tag in the sky translates as "Art is the staff of life."[16]

Hollar moved from Prague to the staunchly Protestant Stuttgart , where he remained until 1629. During his stay it is possible that he met other young artists who had settled there, including Johann Heinrich Schonfeld, Johann Wilhem Baur, and Karel Skreta, a fellow Bohemian. Denkstein has pointed to a convergence of interest between Hollar and Baur, noting the latter's fondness for etching stormy seas and tempests. Hollar made a number of drawings of Stuttgart and its environs, which are still rather stilted in character, and he must have realized that the town was too small to permit him to advance his career.

Sometime in 1629 he moved to Strasbourg, staying there for at least a year and using the city as a springboard for trips to other German towns, including Cologne. It was in Strasbourg that he seriously commenced his profession, and where he undertook his first commissions for print publishers. The half-hearted mannerism of his Prague years was abandoned in favor of a more factual and sober style devoted primarily to topography and also, significantly, to studies of costume. He evidently looked back on his Strasbourg years with affection, because drawings made there in 1629 were being etched in London as late as 1665. His most ambitious drawing, which does not survive, may well have been that which served as the basis for the beautiful etching *Strasbourg Cathedral* (no. 83), which he made in Antwerp in 1645. Allowing a drawing to mature for years before committing it to copper was characteristic of the artist. His drawings constituted a reference library that could be consulted at leisure and with hindsight. In all his numerous moves his drawings must have been the first items to be packed, and the surviving sheets can be but a tiny fragment of the stock that once existed.[17]

Hollar's Strasbourg publisher, Jacob van der Heyden, was presumably responding to popular demand by commission-

3. Jan van de Velde. *Ver*. Etching. British Museum, London.

4. Claesz Jan Visscher. *Haarlem*. Etching. British Museum.

ing copies of Jan van de Velde's sets *Four Seasons* and *Twelve Months*. This was fairly junior employment but largely beyond the powers of the young Hollar; in translation, Van de Velde's crisp lines became rather muddy, with a consequent loss of space and definition. It was a valuable exercise nonetheless, enabling Hollar to concentrate on an artist who was a significant influence on him (fig. 3). Knowledge of prints by the first generation of Dutch artists was crucial to Hollar's development, informing him that gentle everyday landscapes, humble villages even, were fit subjects for an artist and, moreover, salable. With their placid mood and careful composition—fences scissoring up the space, foregrounds carefully separated from backgrounds—Claesz Janz Visscher's *Pleasant Spots,* eleven landscapes published in a set in about 1610, probably had a direct influence on Hollar (fig. 4). The motto that Visscher directed at his potential clients could, with small changes, have been intended for Hollar's later clientele: "The pleasant spots here you can contemplate with ease, devotees who have no time to travel far. Situated outside the agreeable city of Haarlem or thereabouts. Buy without thinking for too long."[18]

Hollar rapidly evolved a delicate technique that employed careful modulations of acid bites; he eschewed the regular grammar of burin work that was still evident in Van de Velde's work. Van der Heyden published the series *Four Seasons* (no. 3), views of Strasbourg that are among Hollar's most beautiful early prints. The most satisfactory plates of the series, *Ver* and

Aestas, deploy expansive horizontal subjects that match the typical Dutch plate format. Hollar closely stuck to the preparatory drawing for *Ver,* which is at Prague, but with one signifi-cant change: the long hedge in the foreground, which acts as a boundary to the shooting range, has been raised, thus focusing the area through which the guns will fire. The design is manifestly sharpened, and such an adjustment, a tightening of pictorial nuts and bolts, is typical of the artist. The first drawing from the subject was a first negotiating position for Hollar, who was always prepared to sacrifice strict fidelity to his model for improved design.[19] Common to all four plates is a certain gentleness of contour, perhaps in reaction to the more determined outlines of Van de Velde. Also notable is the beauty of the lettering beneath the designs, its looping calligraphy af-fording a complement to the more regular lines of the landscape. For Hollar, lettering was never an afterthought or a tedious descriptive necessity but an integral part of the design, a finishing touch in which he evidently delighted.

It is almost certain that Hollar spent part of 1631 in Frankfurt working in the studio of Matthaeus Merian. The most pertinent document for ascertaining the order of his post-Prague movements is a set of landscape etchings entitled *Amoenissimae Effigies* (nos. 11–12), published in Cologne in 1635. The subjects, beginning with Prague, are seemingly arranged in the order in which Hollar visited them. Thus Hollar visited Nuremberg and Augsburg before moving to

5. Rembrandt van Rijn. *Naked Woman Seated on a Mound*. Etching. Yale University Art Gallery. Gift of Lydia Evans Tunnard.

Hollar's main preoccupation in Cologne was with land-scape and costume, and the River Rhine is a leitmotif in the prints and drawings of these years. The river afforded not only the fastest but also the safest means of travel, and the evidence of his prints shows that Hollar must have traveled on the river at least once. He delighted in riverside incidents and became something of a connoisseur of the different types of small craft that frequented the river. In 1634 he followed the Rhine to Amsterdam, and he captured his first enraptured sight of the sea in the wide-eyed little etching *Three Waves* (no. 8). He was able for the first time to study large oceangoing ships, yet he was as interested in work-a-day scenes in the dockyards as he was in the sight of ships in full sail. Hollar was a rational man instinctively drawn to order, which he found *in excelsis* in the functional rigging and bowsprits of ships. He was an innovative master in the competitive genre of the marine print, a fact that is sometimes overlooked. During this visit he made the drawings that served for the set *Dutch Ships* (no. 81) published in Antwerp in 1647.

Hollar visited various towns in Holland, including Rotterdam and Delft, and made studies on the Zuyder Zee. He was as engrossed in the shape of sand dunes outside Amsterdam as he was in the spires of the city itself, and the broad, flat country-side must have recommended itself to the budding artist of panoramas. We have little knowledge of his contact with Dutch artists, though such contact would have been unavoid-able, even in small towns. On the evidence of two prints, how-ever, he was impressed by the etchings of Rembrandt, then aged twenty-seven and already very successful. Hollar copied his 1634 etching *Bust of Saskia* (nos. 9 and 10) in the same year, and in 1635 copied the 1631 work *Naked Woman Seated on a Mound*, a bovine and sagging figure that is among the least appealing and deliberately provocative of Rembrandt's nudes (fig. 5). Hollar evidently appreciated the harsh realism of the nude and Rembrandt's aggressive rejection of the mores of both classical and mannerist art. In both plates Rembrandt is prominently acknowledged, and it is a moot point whether Hollar sought the Dutchman's permission to copy his work. Rembrandt was certainly aware of Hollar, as the inventory of his possessions, drawn up on his insolvency in 1656, itemizes an "East Indian Basket containing several prints by Rembrandt, Hollar, Cocq and several others." Nowhere else in the inventory are prints by Rembrandt listed, and it is possible that a hurried clerk mistook prints by Hollar after Rembrandt for prints by Rembrandt himself.[22]

Stuttgart, then to Strasbourg, and then to Frankfurt, which makes an appearance in plate 14. Cologne and other German cities follow, and the series ends with marine views made in Holland.[20]

Merian's workshop was the hub of print publishing in Germany, and its large output encompassed landscapes, portraits, and the large bird's-eye views of cities for which Merian was best known and from which Hollar had most to learn.[21] Merian's landscapes, which are wild and romantic, must have reeked to Hollar of the effusions of Sadeler in contrast with the simplicity of the new Dutch art. The bird's-eye views were another matter, however. To meet their technical demands it was necessary for an artist to absorb instruction, above all in perspective. Much of Hollar's work in the studio was no doubt mechanical and not acknowledged; but he was allowed to sign *Capture of the Town of Oppenheim,* an undated work that was surely issued soon after the event, which took place on 7 November 1631.

Hollar incorporated *Bust of Saskia* into the series of little etchings published in Cologne in 1636 under the title *Reisbuchlein* ("Little Travel Book"). Saskia's fluffy hair and natural pose contrast oddly with the rather stiff features and static postures of the other women in the series, whose ruffs and fine lace are drawn with more assurance than are their features. The book also contains three busts of men (no. 13), one of them smiling pleasantly. There seems no reason to dispute the traditional identification of the sitter with the artist himself, a resemblance to the man in the Meyssens portrait being very marked. This set was published by Abraham Hogenberg, who also published *Amoenissimae* and a number of other works by Hollar, including the delightful *Bowing Gentleman* and *Lady with a Houpette* (no. 15), his first important full-length costume plates.

Hollar's excursions from Cologne took him also to Mainz, where he made a panoramic view of the city—the first surviving example of this specialty—in which the lessons of Merian were fully absorbed.[23] He evidently spent considerable time in the neighboring town of Düren making drawings for a bird's-eye view that he later etched. A number of drawings of Düren survive, and not all are connected with the bird's-eye view. He apparently drew the other views on the spot, his free penwork enhanced by loosely applied gray washes that suggest light and atmosphere (no. 5).

The seminal event in Hollar's life was the arrival of the Earl of Arundel in Cologne on 2 May 1636. In a letter to his friend and agent, the Reverend William Petty, Arundel noted with satisfaction that "I haue one Hollarse wth me whoe drawes and eches Printes in strong water quickely, and with a pretty spirite."[24] Cologne was the first port of call for Arundel and his extensive retinue on his important embassy to the Emperor Ferdinand II in Vienna. This mission, set in train by Charles I, was intended to restore peace in Europe and, more specifically, to allow Arundel to negotiate with the emperor some restitution to the family of Elizabeth of Palatinate lands lost at the Battle of the White Mountain. Even Arundel was openly pessimistic concerning his chances of success, however. Whether Hollar had offered his services to Arundel or whether Arundel had sought him out is not known, but the meeting was in any case felicitous for both. For Hollar it represented not only secure and interesting employment by a mighty Englishman—one of the greatest collectors of the age (fig. 6)—but also an escape from the increasingly ravaged mainland of Europe. Arundel in turn obtained the services of

an artist who could record the events of the embassy (his rapid execution evidently a point in his favor) and who could, in the longer term, etch copies of some of the works in Arundel's enormous collection.

A factual but turgid account of the embassy was written by William Crowne, who makes no mention of Hollar.[25] Aubrey informs us, however, that "when the Lord Marshall went Ambassador to the Emperor of Germany to Vienna, he travelld with much grandeur; and among others, Mr Hollar went with him (very well clad) to take viewes, landskapes, buildings, etc. remarqueable in their Journey, which we see now at the Print-Shopps."[26] It would seem then, on the basis of Aubrey's characteristic aside, that Hollar's first act to mark his good fortune was to buy a set of new clothes. Hollar's celebrated watercolors, worked up from drawings made on the spot, constitute a record of the embassy's leisurely progress down the Rhine and the Danube in commodious rented boats, on the deckhouses of which curious Englishmen perched like birds on a dovecote. The river was not merely the most convenient mode of transport, it was also the only safe one, as the woods and villages on each side were crawling with bands of ferocious renegade soldiers—the Croats being particularly feared. Hollar told Aubrey that the most celebrated man of the party, William Harvey, a scientist whose work established the principle of the circulation of blood, caused Arundel particular concern by continually wandering into the woods to collect specimens, oblivious to the danger.[27] Horrors were to be found everywhere: starving peasants fighting for the food thrown to them from the boat, unburied corpses with mouths full of grass, villages reduced to ashes.[28] In many of the towns they passed, gunfire could be heard, and even a party as large and prestigious as Arundel's had its moments of nervousness. This is scarcely evident from Hollar's drawings, which are calm and placid, the occasional puffs of gunsmoke seeming as innocuous as fireworks. Hollar was probably aware of Callot's etchings of *Miseries of War*, published in 1633, and although he evidently admired Callot's work—even copying some of his prints of beggars—he had no desire to emulate him. Violence was inimical to Hollar; so far from being a mirror to his age, he simply diverted his gaze from that which was ugly and threatening.

The drawings made on the embassy constitute the largest and most coherent category among his remaining drawings, and they number more than one hundred sheets. They range from rapid graphite notations, such as those in the John

6. Peter Paul Rubens. *Thomas Howard, Earl of Arundel.* Brush and brown and black ink, brown and gray wash heightened with white, with touches of red. Sterling and Francine Clark Art Institute, Williamstown, Massachusetts.

Rylands Library sketchbook, to carefully finished and inscribed watercolors, the finest group being that preserved at Chatsworth (nos. 16–22). The watercolors are of a uniform oblong format, and though some bear dates that correspond to the days when the embassy was at the place depicted, it is more likely that they were executed later, perhaps in England, from the sketches made plein air. Hollar predictably allows himself adjustments of scale and topography to enhance the design of the finished drawings. These drawings surely were intended as an independent series, not as preparations for

prints, and it is difficult to think of any recipient of the drawings other than Arundel himself. It seems likely that the production of such a series was part of Hollar's mandate when he joined the embassy.

The drawings have the character more of tinted drawings than of fully polychromatic watercolors, blue tints being reserved for the hills and buildings and a sparse ration of gray and earth tones for the banks and other foreground features. This use of color accords with the practice of earlier topographical draftsmen, such as Roelandt Savery. The rigging of the lumpen boats provides an opportunity for looping rhythms of form. The penwork of the landscape is rounded and formal, but there is generally little attempt to suggest atmosphere, except in works like *View of Eltville* (no. 20), which is brushed in with cool, moist tints.

Hollar's subject is the river, though he occasionally focuses on a building or group of figures. It is churlish, perhaps, but one would willingly forsake a few of the landscape sketches for a costume study or a sketch of William Harvey rambling in the woods. The mood of these works is placid save for the exceptional image *A Public Execution at Linz* (no. 27), in which Hollar lifts the curtain from the horrors that he normally avoided. A large crowd, raptly attentive, witness rebellious peasants being hacked to pieces on a scaffold in the city square. At the lower right edge of the crowd a well-dressed woman grins like the Cheshire cat. Such a scene, familiar enough in Callot, is unexpected in Hollar, and it is the more disturbing for the pragmatism of Hollar's vision, which is concerned as much with the technical problem of drawing a host of people as with reacting to the bloody shambles he has witnessed.[29]

The embassy proceeded in great state from city to city, arriving in Vienna at the end of June and leaving for Prague at the beginning of July. The party remained in Prague for a week, giving the artist time to impress his family and friends with his new station—not to mention the fine raiment so essential among the English of that time. Crowne's leaden prose does not enlighten us, but it seems likely that Hollar was a member of the group shown around the Treasury, containing Rudolf's Cabinet, which held such curiosities as a "Unicorn's Horn, one yard long," and a cupboard containing "basins, ewers and cups all made of amber." Hollar, perhaps conscious that another opportunity may not come, spent much time on drawings of the city, which he later used for his celebrated *Great Prospect of Prague*.[30]

Ultimately Arundel's mission proved politically fruitless. But he had known from the outset (as had his cynical critics) that the course of diplomacy would yield opportunities to the collector. And so it was, as towns vied with one another to present gifts to such a famous connoisseur. Thus in Düsseldorf the Duke of Neuburg "had made arrangements to entertain His Excellency at his house, but realizing that His Excellency preffered to avoid delay, he sent for a wild boar, wine, and five pictures, all of which he presented to His Excellency."[31] Arundel's prime requirement as a collector was a paint-

ing by Dürer, but here he was disappointed, writing to William Petty, then in Venice searching for artworks for Arundel, that in Nuremberg he had found a "most miserable Countrye, and nothing by ye way to be bought at any momente, heer in this towne beinge not one scratch of Alb:Duerer's paintinge in oyle to be sold, though it were his Countrye, no of Holbein nor other great men."[32] It must have been doubly frustrating for him when the city of Nuremberg entrusted him with two important Dürer paintings to present to Charles I. He did, however, have the ample consolation of purchasing the library of Dürer's greatest friend, Willibald Pirckheimer.[33]

The embassy returned through Holland and spent eight days at The Hague, mainly at the court of the exiled queen of Bohemia. The group landed in Deal on 27 December, and the odyssey finally came to an end the next day when the party traveled to London by barge from Gravesend. It was appropriate that the river, which was to become one his favored subjects, afforded Hollar his first sight of London and his first glimpse of a country that was at peace.

HOLLAR'S FIRST ENGLISH PERIOD

At the age of twenty-nine Hollar began his career in England. The Germany that he left behind him—smoldering, ruinous, fetid with pestilence—would have been unlikely to offer many opportunities, and if he had stayed it is doubtful that he would now occupy more than a few dim pages of Hollstein's illustrated volumes. But by the time he reached England he was a skilled but conservative etcher and a first-class topographer, though as a watercolorist he was limited to the use of three or four colors. He was a fine draftsman of costume, but he had not mastered figure drawing, and he had problems explaining in lines the structure of a head. His two copies of Rembrandt etchings had proved him an able copyist, and he was a master on a small scale, a talent highly amenable to English taste. His personality was such that he must have soon made friends; Aubrey describes him as a "very friendly good natured man as could be," and Francis Place told George Vertue that "Mr. Hollar was a very passionate man easily moved. . . . he has often told me, he was always uneasie if not at work. he was one of great temperance I don't think in all his life was ever seen in drink. but wou'd eat very heartily."[34]

For a young artist independent of family ties, employment in England under its premier earl was one of the greatest

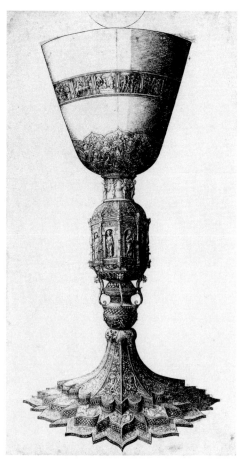

7. Fifteenth-Century Venetian. *Design for a Chalice.* Pen and brown ink on vellum. British Museum, London.

8. Jan Lievens. *Jacques Gaultier.* Etching. British Museum, London.

blessings that contemporary patronage could bestow.[35] It is probable that Hollar was at first accommodated in Arundel House, a ramshackle collection of buildings facing the Strand on one side and the river on the other. Arundel's princely collection was housed here, and in 1636 the most notable embellishment had been the long sculpture gallery running almost the length of the main building. This gallery housed Arundel's collection of antique marbles, which was of international renown.[36] On 1 January 1637, a party was held to mark the opening of a brand-new room to house the vast collection of prints and drawings.[37] The house overflowed with paintings: lordly canvases by Rubens and Van Dyck; the greatest assemblage of Holbeins ever made; sublime Titians, including the *Three Ages of Man,* and the *Flaying of Marsyas,* which, perhaps mercifully, Hollar never tried to copy. Yet Arundel also delighted in the small pictures of Jan Brueghel and the jewel-like pictures on copper by Adam Elsheimer. The collection of drawings was equally grand, containing many of the Leonardo drawings that are now at Windsor.[38]

It was a principal part of Hollar's employment to make drawings of objects in the collection and later transcribe the drawings into etchings (fig. 7; no. 38). Etching was scarcely known in England, and the only serious practitioners had been such foreigners as Marcus Gheeraerts or Jan Lievens, whose bristling portraits of the centenarian Robert South (no. 49) and court lutenist Jacques Gaultier (fig. 8) are among the finest etchings ever made in England. Lievens had left England for Antwerp in 1634, so Hollar's gentler art did not invite comparison.[39] The field, therefore, was entirely his.

The native tradition of line engraving was threadbare and provincial, bereft even of the charm of simplicity. It too had relied largely on the efforts of foreigners, such as the De Passe family, and it consists mainly of endless grim faces peering out from elaborate surrounds. Its poverty was such that even the meanest English talents were able to make a living by scratching portraits of clerics to front their volumes of sermons or executing the emblematic frontispieces in which people of the age delighted.[40] The only engraver of promise was William Faithorne (no. 124), who in 1637 was still working in the dazzling curvilinear manner of the fashionable French engraver Claude Mellan.[41]

The terms of Hollar's employment were evidently easy, and he was free to spend time etching and publishing subjects unrelated to the Arundel collection on his own account. The first great print of his English period, *Greenwich* of 1637 (no.

32), was thus dedicated to Queen Henrietta Maria, though the artist was at pains to style himself Arundel's "Coelator." This expansive design, etched on two plates, is a stunning declaration of intent and a landscape of a grandeur and sophistication never before seen in England. The focal point, in the middle distance, is the Queen's House, which Inigo Jones had finished only in 1635. London can be seen in the background, and in the foreground Hollar has indulged his propensity for long, flowing curved lines, which move with leisurely state from the Royal Observatory at the left, down to a central plateau, and then up and beyond to another great, barrowlike hill. It is a motion to be savored, and it is rendered the sweeter by the inclusion of two fashionable women who move slowly against the flow of the lines, which seem molded and rollered for human perambulation. The print breathes a sense of peace and contentment of mind; it is a high point of Hollar's art, and it stands with Van Dyck's watercolor landscapes as one of the foundation stones of the English landscape tradition. Hollar's penchant for "taking a line for a walk" is also much in evidence in another early print, *Richmond Palace* (no. 33), etched in two nearly identical versions in 1638.

Two more dedicatory prints exist from these early years when Hollar was seeking to establish his credentials. The large, highly finished etching of *Seleucus and His Son* (no. 35) had particular significance because of its dedication to Arundel. Based on a design by Guilio Romano, its theme is one of paternal fidelity and stoic virtue (fig. 9). The son of Seleucus, a governor in the Greek Empire, was accused of adultery; for punishment he was to be blinded. But Seleucus saved one of his son's eyes by offering to sacrifice one of his own. The Latin text that urges us to take heed of this austere virtue was by the then decrepit Henry Peacham, once tutor to Arundel's children, who provided Latin texts for a number of Hollar prints.[42] This important print raises a number of interesting questions. Who chose such a subject? Did Arundel direct Hollar to copy this drawing, an assumption made by David Howarth, Arundel's most recent biographer?[43] Was the selection perhaps a diplomatic choice by the artist himself, guided by a learned adviser, such as Peacham? Or was the selection made in consultation between patron and artist? It is possible that Hollar had more autonomy of choice than many commentators have allowed him.

Of equal significance is another dedicatory print, the carefully finished 1639 etching of the so-called *Wilton Diptych*, a fourteenth-century masterpiece that entered the collection of

9. Sixteenth-century Italian school. *Seleucus and His Son.* Pen and wash. After Guilio Romano. British Museum, London.

Charles I in that year (fig. 10; no. 37). It is to the king himself that the print is dedicated. Hollar here had an eye to his own notice and advancement and was relying on the king's knowledge of his own dynastic history. The subject and probable patron of the painting is the ill-starred Richard II, who is depicted kneeling before the Virgin. Hollar's interest was surely aroused by the fact that Richard's first queen, Anne, was the daughter of the Emperor Charles IV, King of Bohemia. Hollar makes her ancestry clear in his text, thereby drawing attention to himself, prominently lettering his name and Bohemian nationality. He was even at pains to etch the plate in the same direction as the picture, the practice he always adopted when drawing from landscape or townscape, but scarcely ever when copying pictures or drawings.[44]

There is no evidence that the king had the slightest interest in works on paper, but it is some measure of his acceptance of Hollar that in about 1640 he was appointed drawing master to the Prince of Wales, the future Charles II, though the post may well have been fairly nominal.[45] A further suggestion of royal favor is found in the presence of a privilege—a rudimentary form of copyright—on a number of plates made between 1638 and 1642. For example, "Cum Priuilegio Sacr; Regae; Majestatis" is inscribed on *The Wilton Diptych*. Such an inscription was obligatory in France but unusual in England. It is used too erratically in Hollar's work, however, to act as evidence that he had an actual monopoly on certain works.[46]

10. Unknown artist of the fourteenth century. *The Wilton Diptych.* Tempera and gold leaf on panel. National Gallery, London.

It is evident that Hollar was spending more time with his sketchbook than in his etching studio. Only a fraction of his drawings were etched before his enforced departure to Antwerp in 1644, where he completed many works begun in England, including a number from the Arundel collection. Our understanding of Hollar's work as copyist for Arundel is unlikely ever to be complete, but it is possible that Arundel hoped for an etched and engraved record of masterpieces from his collection, perhaps to be published in book form. This would have supplemented John Selden's *Marmora Arundeliana* of 1628, which compiled the classical transcriptions from antique marbles but lacked illustrations. Hollar and his colleague Hendrick van der Borcht were not the first artists to copy drawings in the collection; they had been preceded by the Flemish engraver Lucas Vorsterman.[47] Such a project obviously would have taken far longer than the troubled politics of Stuart England would allow. Hollar's copies were confined almost entirely to drawings and paintings; his one attempt at copying a marble figure was a woebegone failure.[48] If indeed Arundel was giving general guidance to his artists, as must surely have been the case, it must have been evident to him that Hollar's gift was linear and tonal. Hollar had, however,

little experience drawing naked figures from life or from the antique, and perhaps he was sensibly advised to leave the marbles to their own devices.

Hollar's approach to reproductive etching is an individual one, and it is a mistake to regard his work as wholly faithful to the originals. This dictum may be applied to his work in general. He is not an impersonal "mirror to his age." He is rather an enlightening but sometimes idiosyncratic guide. He seldom troubled to retain the original direction of the works he copied, but he redressed this shortcoming in part by printing numerous counterproofs. In some cases, such as the tiny pictures by Elsheimer (nos. 70–71) or Leonardo's *Five Grotesque Old Men* (no. 66), his copies are exceptionally faithful. In many other cases, this most rational-minded of artists was moved to improve designs to remedy defects, to tidy up, complete, and elucidate areas he found unclear. Thus a damaged area of *The Wilton Diptych* is neatly prepared, an angel's arm and wing filled out. The complexities of a windowsill in Dürer's *Self-Portrait* are geometrically simplified, and the arms of Dürer's father are given an extra contour lacking in the original. Mary Giggs, drawn three-quarter length by Holbein, retains only her head in Hollar's little print. A distressing number of paintings and drawings copied by Hollar are now lost; if any should surface, their authenticity should not necessarily be disputed because of slight discrepancies between them and the Bohemian's print—in fact, the discrepancies may work to confirm the drawings' authenticity. Hollar's lovingly etched copies of Elsheimer's tiny paintings are frequently quite faithful to the original, but his print of *Latona* (no. 69), a picture rediscovered by Keith Andrews, contains several variations from the original.[49] Likewise, in copies of drawings by Leonardo and Holbein he could show fidelity to his models, yet he would sometimes combine elements from several sheets to make a single etched design.[50]

The patronage of Arundel, the approval of the king, the benefaction of marriage in 1640 to Mistress Tracey, lady-in-waiting to the Countess of Arundel, made this the most benign period of Hollar's life. One advantage, however, eluded him—the approbation of Sir Anthony Van Dyck. Van Dyck was the star in the firmament of Caroline art, and although Hollar etched numerous Van Dyck portraits, the etchings were mainly done after the painter's death in 1642, and the results are often lamentable. Van Dyck had been brought up in the tradition of Rubens, and his school of dynamic reproductive engraving, with the swelling engraved lines achieved by Vorsterman and others rehearsing the baroque motions of the paintings. Van Dyck's own unfinished portrait etchings for *Iconographie* (no. 48) exploit the freedom of the etching needle to create rapid changes and motion in pose.[51] This was foreign to Hollar, something of a seamstress of the etcher's trade, who had scarcely a baroque flourish in his repertoire. Nonetheless, with Van Dyck dead, he ventured to etch the latter's *Self-Portrait with the Sunflower* (no. 47), and the print's importance may be gauged by its dedication to John Evelyn. Yet, all claims to fidelity thrust aside, he straightens up the baroque tilt of Van Dyck's head, changes the petals of the flowers, alters the format, and transmits a radical reinterpretation of the original that the painter surely would never have sanctioned.

A degree of familiarity with Van Dyck is suggested, however, by the fact that Hollar was John Aubrey's informant for the knowledge that Van Dyck's mistress, Margaret Lemon, was "a dangerous woman" and "a demon of jealousy who caused the most horrible scenes when ladies belonging to London society had been sitting, without chaperone, to her lover for their portraits."[52] Further evidence that Hollar had entrée to Van Dyck's studio and, seemingly, license to make sketches, is

revealed by some of the prints of *Ornatus Muliebris* (no. 41), a series of twenty-six etchings of women in varied attire. The etchings were begun in 1638 and published in 1640. These beautifully clad women, without the grandeur of Van Dyck but not without state, parade the Caroline ravishments of their costume in a carefully ordered and rotated sequence of poses. Ladies of the court in glistening silk dresses compete for attention with severely attired city women. In this array, we can find at least four women deftly abstracted by Hollar from Van Dyck's canvases; they are reversed by the printing to disguise the theft but are still recognizable. Thus the portrait of Lady Mary Villiers (fig. 11), now in the North Carolina Museum of Art, is reversed and shamelessly claimed for the Hollarean world.[53]

11. Sir Anthony Van Dyck. *Mary Villiers, Duchess of Lennox and Richmond.* Oil on canvas. North Carolina Museum of Art, Raleigh. Gift of Mrs. Theodore Webb.

Hollar adored women—the complexities of their hair, their posture, and their clothing and accessories, their fur muffs being to his special delectation. This enraptured contemplation of the feminine world is the best-loved aspect of his work, and one in which he transcends plain prose and draws and etches with poetic spirit. In this he is at one with such courtly poets as Herrick, Lovelace, or Suckling, who vie for our attention with their verses in praise of female beauty.

Engraving and high fashion went arm in arm from the very beginnings of the art. The Master of the Playing Cards, active in the Upper Rhineland in the 1440s, delighted in plump young men in fluffy scalloped cloaks. Fifteenth-century Florentine engravings teem with fashionably dressed figures who are as at home in sacred subjects as they are in erotic allegories. Israel van Meckenem, Albrecht Dürer, Lucas van Leyden, and Hendrick Goltzius plucked themes almost at random from their reference books as a pretext for glorified fashion plates. In his own time, Hollar was aware of the strutting homunculi of Callot's *Capricci* and the fops of Abraham Bosse (no. 45). He was also conversant with the long history of prints devoted to the costumes of different countries. Some of the best known were Jost Amman's woodcuts, which were published at the end of the sixteenth century under the title *Habitus Praecipuorem Populorem*. In fact this was reissued in Ulm as late as 1639 when Hollar was busy with the little plates of his *Aula Veneris*. The title to the second edition of Amman's *Gynaeceum . . . Theatrum Mulierum* explains that the work is illustrated both to extol the female sex and to "benefit most of all those who are unable to travel because of their lifestyle or of some other reasons who in their home occasionally take delight in different people's regional costume, which is a tacit indication of character."

Such a purpose is central to Hollar's *Aula Veneris* (no. 42), the first part of which was published in London in 1643 and then was constantly reissued in various forms until 1816. This series was long in the making. Hollar had been gathering material since his early German years, and even though the prints are dated between 1642 and 1649, many of the drawings used must have been made much earlier. Hollar's subjects, full of charm and variety of pose, range from homely Londoners to a half-naked Virginian, and the series was obviously aimed at an international market.

The most ambitious and imposing of the costume prints are the stately women of *The Four Seasons* (no. 44), etched in 1643 and 1644. The women are standing on raised platforms, dwarf-ing the beautiful landscapes and townscapes beyond, the contours of their garments mapped against the clear sky with a topographer's eye to rhythm and variety. Their shoes and the hems of their skirts gently debate precedence with the ruled border line below. Most celebrated is the figure of *Winter*, who is eyeing us knowingly from behind her mask and bunching up her skirts. The verses beneath proclaim:

> The cold not cruelty makes her ware
> In Winter Furre and Wild Beasts Haire
> For a smoother skinn at night
> Embraceth her with more delight

It is the prerogative of the topographer to show us nature free of encumbrances, and architecture presenting its ideal aspect. Smoke thus plays but a small part in Hollar's work. Yet if John Evelyn in his furious essay *Fumifugium* is to be believed, and surely he is, Hollar would have smelt London before he saw it: "And what is all this, but the Hellish and dismall Cloud of SEA COALE. . . . It is this horrid smoake which obscures our churches, and makes our palaces look old, which fouls our clothes, and corrupts the waters. . . . It is this which diffuses and spreads a Yellownesse upon our choycest pictures and hangings." Evelyn assures us that the spotless white lace collars of Hollar's women would have been speckled with black within minutes of their exposure to the open air. "How it sticks on the hands, faces and linnen of our fair Ladies, and nicer Dames, who reside constantly in London (especially during winter) the prodigious wast of Almond-powder for the one, soap and wearing out of the other, do sufficiently manifest."[54]

Clothes could not be spread on a bush to dry without acquiring a coating of filth. Flowers and vegetables rotted as soon as they had flourished. Countrymen exposed to the fumes fell sick and died. Indeed, Hollar's London was more the fetid city of Charles Dickens's *Our Mutual Friend* than the clean, contoured place that he depicts. Hollar's intention as a topographer was to clear the air, to show us what should be, and to provide the armchair traveler with pleasure and edification. He scours its surfaces, cleans its gutters, and clips clear the edges of the buildings until we half believe in this idyllic metropolis in which well-clad figures stroll and take their ease.

Lodged in Arundel House, Hollar was confronted daily by the Thames River, the main thoroughfare of the city, onto which faced a number of its grandest buildings. The river, teeming with small craft ferrying passengers, was a subject in which Hollar delighted. The Thames has long been the prerogative of foreign artists, who have viewed its grandeur and activity with fresh eyes. In the 1750s Canaletto gave us a sunlit vision of Wren's City churches dominating the skyline. In the nineteenth century Whistler relished the decaying buildings and forest of masts at Limehouse while Monet painted endless misty views from his vantage point at the Savoy Hotel. In the twentieth century the river inspired Derain and Kokoschka, and it even induced Claes Oldenburg to fantasize a monstrous ball cock that would bob in its changing tidal waters.[55] Hollar's immediate predecessors included Claude de Jongh, a Dutch artist who probably painted his *View at Westminster* (no. 29) from drawings made in London. His is a curious vision, showing London seemingly fossilized, with a man crawling across its stones like an explorer while a shrouded boat creeps at funereal pace across the water.[56]

Hollar particularly relished views up the river, such as the one in *View of Westminster and the Thames from Lambeth House* (no. 31), which shows the long wooden watergates with boats clustered around them, disgorging passengers. He also used the river as a platform from which to view four square august buildings, including those featured in *Whitehall From the River* and *Lambeth Palace* (no. 61). The ruled horizontal lines of the water serve almost as tramlines to the boats and act as a foil to the vertical lines of the unsullied buildings behind. Another aspect of London that engaged him was the proximity of country to town, exemplified in the exquisite *Tothill Fields* (no. 50), in which groups of figures ramble in fields scarcely a stone's throw from Westminster Abbey.

Comparatively few of Hollar's London views were etched and published in England. Most awaited completion in his later years in Antwerp, but he evidently made hundreds of drawings, some of which survive, including a small group of sketches acquired at some time by Samuel Pepys and housed today in the Pepys Library at Cambridge.[57] In spite of the small scale of much of his work, Hollar thought and planned on the grand scale, and it seems likely that from an early stage he was making drawings for the celebrated *Long View of London from Bankside* (no. 62), published in Antwerp in 1647. A handful of these drawings exist, and they suggest that the artist had recourse to high places, such as church spires, from which to make studies of the many Gothic and Tudor structures that clustered around the handful of modern buildings.

In one aspect, and one alone, did English art outshine all other schools, and that was in the art of the miniature. A tra-

dition founded by Holbein and refined in the mannerist Elizabethan elegance of Nicholas Hilliard and Isaac Oliver was in Hollar's time perfected by the supreme naturalism of Samuel Cooper, the "Prince of Limners."[58] It was an art form to which Hollar was deeply sympathetic and that he probably practiced, though no examples now survive. His few unqualified successes as a portraitist are set in the framework of the miniature tradition. Hollar was a prolific portrait etcher, both as a copyist and from drawings made *ad vivum*. He did, however, labor under an unfortunate disadvantage when working from life, namely an almost constitutional inability to distinguish one set of features from another. He seems never to have observed properly the nuances of tone and shading created by a vagary of cheekbone structure, nor the variety of noses and mouths that any random group of people will sport. His faces, in short, are all from the same mold. A similar stricture may be applied to many Stuart or Georgian painters, but in their cases the mold was dictated by fashion and tailored into the barest semblance of a likeness. To Hollar, a variation in a lace ruff, hairstyle, or pendant ribbon was more noticeable than a dimpled chin or a snub nose. That this was a perceived weakness in his lifetime is proved by at least one commissioned plate, that of *Charles II as Prince of Wales,* for which Hollar was paid to etch the landscape background and the costumed figure but was evidently instructed to leave the space for the face blank for another hand to complete (figs. 12A–12B).[59]

The influence of portrait miniatures is most evident in the thirty-seven plates that constitute the *Women's Heads in Circles* (no. 77), not only in their circular format but in their scale and in the directness of confrontation with the sitters. The faces are somewhat generalized and their clothes form the chief object of the exercise, but some appear to be portraits, and one is copied directly from John Hoskins. A number of these heads are also notable for their brilliant lighting, an etched effect peculiar to Hollar's work.

From his arrival in England until 1642 Hollar appears to have been almost entirely independent of the print sellers, his name appearing on the plate alone, though seldom with the addition of *excudit* to show that he was also the publisher. In the absence of other evidence it must be presumed that he kept stocks of his prints in his studio and sold directly to collectors, thus eliminating any need for the middlemen who would play so large a part in his later career.

In 1642, however, this comfortable phase in Hollar's life came to an abrupt end. Aware that civic discord was about to

12. Wenceslaus Hollar. *Charles II as Prince of Wales.* Etching. British Museum, London.

A. First state, before addition of the head.
B. Fifth state, with head of Charles II added by another artist.

A

B

give way to civil war, Arundel obtained permission to travel to Europe, and he moved to Antwerp. He never returned to England. His collections, the raison d'être for Hollar's presence in the household, were also moved to Antwerp, whence traveled their curator, Hendrick van der Borcht. Over the years they were gradually sold and dispersed. Hollar was thus thrown upon his own resources—and into the embrace of the print sellers, who welcomed him with open arms and tightly buttoned wallets. For the rest of his long life he was to remain dependent on booksellers and print sellers, a number of whom figure high in the demonology of Hollar's admirers.

Chief among them was Peter Stent, whose commencement in business in 1642 coincides with Hollar's demise as an independent artist.[60] Hollar's unwonted exposure to the vicissitudes of trade and his lack of business sense was notorious. He was, according to Aubrey, "Shiftlesse to the Worlde." He seems to have been unable or unwilling to take the logical step of publishing his own prints, as William Faithorne did. From this time Hollar had to seek work wherever he could, and as a consequence a large proportion of his work is the product of

drudgery and of little interest. Nor did he have the inclination or organizational ability to take on pupils who could have shouldered a portion of the meaner work. No doubt he was exploited by publishers, especially Stent, but a great deal of money must have passed through his hands in the course of his life, and he was obviously feckless in its disposal. It is difficult to imagine his wife and his daughter ("one of the greatest beauties I have ever seen," according to Aubrey) in any but the finest clothes, and no doubt Hollar's social aspirations carried their own burden of expense.

The shadows of civil war advanced by degree in Hollar's work, first in the military plates occasioned by Arundel's expedition to Scotland at the head of an English army in 1638, which was forced to retreat ignominiously when confronted by a superior Scottish force. Hollar's *Earl of Arundel on Horseback* (no. 53) is a brave but doomed attempt at grand manner portraiture, and Arundel seems as ill at ease in his martial persona as does Hollar with the problems of a rearing horse. Popular demand dictated that Hollar etch numerous maps and portraits of the war and its protagonists. His sympathies were royalist, but he had remained in London, a parliamentarian stronghold, and had, needs be, to etch portraits of the king's enemies. Yet throughout this difficult period he made time to etch plates of more personal interest, including *Seasons* (no. 44), and the first plate of the series *Muffs* (no. 92).

At this difficult time Hollar was looking for new outlets for his work, and his mind went back to his German years. It was not until 1643, surprisingly, that he etched *View of Strasbourg,* which completed the important set of twelve continental views (no. 51). These works, prepared many years before, suggest that Hollar was aware that he might have to look beyond England to market his prints. He also may have been driven by nostalgia, sheer aesthetic motivation, and his compulsion to neatly complete a series. This set is among Hollar's finest achievements. Using the small oblong format favored by Dutch landscape etchers, he concentrated on river views, the crisply ruled skies cut and divided by the spars and rigging of small craft. In a passage especially mellifluous, the etched border line of *Strasbourg: The Toll House* fulfills its function and then branches gently into the design and outlines a bank of earth.

Hollar's most personal and touching contribution to the iconography of the civil war is the remarkable *Comparison of the English and Bohemian Civil Wars* (no. 58), a melancholy reflection on his inability to escape turmoil and conflict. It is also a design of great sophistication, combining abstract shapes and symbols with the naturalism of the sweeping Bohemian plains. It is undated but must have been etched in about 1642. The armed conflict of the war had been preceded by an interminable battle of words in which the rival factions produced scores of vituperative pamphlets and broadsides, frequently issued with crude woodcuts and hurled at their rivals with partisan fury.[61] The futility of this war of words is summed up in Hollar's satirical print *The World is Ruled and Governed by Opinion,* and the sheer viperine nastiness of civil conflict is encapsulated by his crisp little print of *Civilis Seditio* (no. 56).

HOLLAR IN ANTWERP

In 1644, as war raged across the country, Hollar began to settle his affairs in England. He sold a number of his copper plates, including *Long View of Greenwich,* to Peter Stent; Francis Place noted that "Old Peter Stent made an advantage of purchasing several of his plates for a trifle," Hollar receiving a beggarly thirty shillings for one of his most prestigious plates.[62] At some time in this year Hollar gathered together his

drawings and a selection of his etched plates and made his way to Antwerp, a logical destination because it was there that Arundel had taken his collection. By the time Hollar arrived Arundel had retired to Padua, however; even if he had remained it is doubtful whether he could have afforded the artist much protection. The countess, from whom Arundel was largely estranged, remained in Antwerp and subsisted by gradually selling off parts of the collection. It is not known how long Hollar's association with the Arundel household continued. In 1646 he dedicated his print of Dürer's *Woman with Coiled Hair* to the countess, but this gesture was perhaps a courteous reminder of his existence, not evidence of a close connection. Nor do we know whether Hollar had access to the collections; in his eight years in Antwerp he produced many etchings of works of art there, but they could have been made from drawings produced in London. It is evident that Hollar had brought with him his entire stock of drawings, which must by this time have been vast. Those drawings provided a bedrock of material for the next years. Because they included many views of London that Hollar etched in Antwerp, it is a mistake to differentiate too sharply between the London and the Antwerp periods. Hollar had by no means abandoned his English clientele, and his etchings of English views and subjects must have been largely intended for the English market.

From this period date *Views of Arundel House* (no. 60); most of the *Women's Heads in Circles* (no. 77); the much loved and nostalgic *Views of Albury* (no. 59), Arundel's beloved country retreat in Surrey (fig. 13); and the highly wrought little plates of *Muscarum Scarabeorum* (no. 95), which are teeming with exquisitely arranged moths and insects. Most important of all is *Long View of London from Bankside* (no. 62), published by Cornelis Danckers in Amsterdam in 1647. This masterpiece, one of the finest of all panoramic views, is given even greater historical value by the destruction of much of the city in the Great Fire of 1666. Inscribed "Wenceslaus Hollar delineavit et fecit Londini et Antwerpiae," it was etched in Antwerp from the hundreds of drawings he had made in London, of which only a handful survive. He must also have had access to Claesz Janz Visscher's 1616 *Panorama of London,* but the grand scale of Hollar's design, the great stretch of the river as it curves away into the distance, the contrast between sharply defined planes of the roofs on the South Bank with the minuscule details of North London, render Visscher's print tired and obsolete.

Little is documented of these years, save the sheer volume of prints that he made—more than 350, including many large

13. Wenceslaus Hollar. *William Oughtred*. Etching. British Museum, London. Oughtred (1575–1660) was the rector of Albury from 1610 until his death. He was an intimate friend of Arundel's. His book *Key of Mathematics* passed through many editions. John Aubrey said of this portrait, "They say that no *picture* in black and white could be more like a man. There is a cheerful air visible."

and important plates. Hollar's first act on arriving in Antwerp must have been to contact his erstwhile colleague and friend Hendrick van der Borcht, who published a number of Hollar's prints, particularly those associated with the Arundel collection. It is possible that Hollar controlled the sale and distribution of some of his Antwerp prints, but for the most part he was in thrall to various Antwerp publishers. The most important of these publishers were Jan Meyssens and Francis van den Wyngaerde, the latter specializing in reproductive prints after Old Masters. To Meyssens we owe a debt of gratitude for his portrait of Hollar proudly clutching a finished copper plate, the tools of his trade laid out before him.

By the time of his move to Antwerp Hollar's technical powers were at their height, and it was probable that he was stimulated by the greater competition on the Continent. Hollar

has deliberately covered his tracks concerning his technique, and the evidence is mainly to be found in the prints themselves. A few revealing scraps of evidence remain, thus a trial proof (now lost) of his etched copy of Holbein's *Soloman and the Queen of Sheba* had a letter on the back from Hollar to Van der Borcht the elder, which testifies to his perfectionism. "According to the special wish of your son I am forwarding you this proof, made in his presence. Do not think, please, that this is a perfect proof of the print. I have printed it on paper immediately after removing the acid. But in principle after the acid treatment, corrections in the plate must be done. In this case, however, they were omitted. I am therefore rather reluctant to send you the proof. I never send proofs away until they are perfect. Here in this case you can only notice and see what the acid has done, but it hasn't been touched by the needle."[63]

Trial proofs must have been numerous, but Hollar obviously destroyed most of them, and they are now of the greatest rarity.[64] It is probable that Hollar finished a plate with an engraving burin rather than a needle, and a burin, with its characteristic wooden mushroom handle, is visible on the table in the Meyssens portrait.

Richard Symonds, an English traveler and antiquary, gives us a glimpse into the etcher's studio, which he visited on 20 February 1649. He wrote in his notebook that "I saw Mr Hollar etching & he laid on the water wch cost him 4s pound & was not half a quarter of an hour eating. it bubled presently. he stird it with a feather. he lays on the wax with a clout & smooths it with a feather. he makes a Verge to keep in the water after it is cutt with yellow wax & Tallow mellted together & layd it on wth a pencil he always Stirs the Aqua with a feather."[65] This passage is infuriatingly abbreviated, omitting to tell us which plate Hollar was etching, but nonetheless it affords us vital information about his technical procedures. Seventeenth-century etchers adopted one of two methods. The first involved holding the plate at an angle and pouring the acid over it, whence it splashed down into a receptacle. The second (as described by Symonds) involved building an acid-resistant wall around the copper, which itself served as the base to this miniature dam. The latter method allowed the etcher to control the biting process with greater care. It is evident from the description that Hollar was using a powerful nitric acid, which bites strong lines quickly and forms bubbles that need to be cleared by a feather—a homely tool still in use today. A gentler acid, usually described as a mordant, which does not raise bubbles, would be used for more delicate passages. The intricacy of some of Hollar's plates must have required a whole series of potentially hazardous immersions in the acid, as did the more elaborate of Rembrandt's plates. Simpler plates may have required only one immersion. The length of time required to bite to the correct depth could be learned only through experience, and by the occasional disasters that have added gray hairs to the heads of all etchers.

Hollar's justly celebrated etchings of fur muffs (no. 92) are his most personal contribution to the history of printmaking, and they show his technical achievement at its summit. The first was etched in London in 1640, and the last and most splendid was completed in Antwerp in 1647. They had appeared with their personable owners in the fashion series, of course, but composing them into still life groups was wholly original—as was the very idea of making still life a genre appropriate to original printmaking.

An ability to paint fur was almost mandatory for the portrait painters of Northern Europe, and it was a test of technical virtuosity. The pinched faces of Van Eyck's sitters are protected by fur collars, as are the anxious sitters of Holbein. For Venetian painters, such as Titian and Lotto, the fur stoles of

their subjects were more a luxurious adornment than a practical necessity, and Rubens and Van Dyck painted fur with a similar joyousness—and frank sensuousness in the case of Rubens' portrait of Helene Fourment, naked save for her fur wrapping.

But in the graphic arts there was small precedent for the subject, let alone in the form of muffs. A number of Rembrandt's etched portraits, such as *Jan Sylvius* and the so-called *Oriental Heads,* show sitters sporting fur stoles and coats, but the artist scarcely differentiates between the texture of fur and that of the shaggy, ratty locks of his sitters. A fur-clad woman is found in Leonard Bramer's etching *Lute Player,* and the luxury of her costume forms part of an assemblage of Vanitas objects.

The spirit of Hollar's work is, however, anything but cautionary; indeed, there was little of the moralist about him. Hollar's *Muffs* demonstrate the sophistication of his art. They are sensual, sexual even, and the delight of the artist in his subject is unashamedly obsessional.[66]

The other masterpiece of the Antwerp years is the unpublished series *Shells* (no. 93). The crystallized lines that define their hard, brittle surfaces are a direct complement to the softness of the muffs. It is a matter of regret that he never com-

14. Emmanuel de Critz. *John Tradescant the Younger with His Collection of Shells.* Oil on canvas. Ashmolean Museum, Oxford.

bined the two subjects in a single plate. The works in the series are neither signed nor dated, but it is likely that they were etched in Antwerp. In the seventeenth century shells were esteemed and collected as curiosities of nature, and a collection of fine specimens was part of the Cabinet of many collectors. Shells were frequently the subject of still life paintings like those by Balthaser van Alst, and they were often, by reason of their petrified fragility, a Vanitas component on which the spectator was invited to contemplate the brevity and fragility of life (fig. 14).[67]

Pennington records thirty-eight plates, the same number found by Vertue in "a most curious Book of Shells, in Thirty Eight Plates. Some of the Plates have Letters of Reference, most of them have none. Many Collectors of Hollar's Works have them not; nor are they to be met with in the most numerous Collections, except Two or Three, where they are esteemed as great rarities."[68] To this number may be added the unrecorded print in this catalogue (no. 93F), but it should be noted that at least one print in the series is not by Hollar.

They etchings are certainly not intended as Vanitas objects, but otherwise their purpose remains unclear, though it is to be presumed that the artist intended his manifest labor to result in a published set. This did not happen, and the great rarity of all the prints suggests that he lost control of the plates at an early date, even, perhaps, by accident. They are marvels of form and space—some are monumental, others seem to float in space like asteroids, and others sport rococo twists and turns of contour. They are, above all, about etching, and their microscopic fineness of line, sometimes augmented by burin work, has seldom been equaled. Rembrandt's famous etching *Shell* (no. 94) was probably drawn from an example in his own collection, but it may well have been etched in a spirit of emulation of Hollar's work, particularly in the first state, before the introduction of dense shadows. Like Hollar's work it transcends any narrow definition of scientific illustration, but his introduction of cast shadows emphasizes Hollar's boldness in presenting his subjects so unadorned.[69]

Other important prints of this period include the monumental *Antwerp Cathedral* (no. 86) and one of his best crowd scenes, *The Peace of Munster* (no. 85). One significant set of prints that must be singled out from the Antwerp years is the twelve-plate series of *Navium variae figurae et formae*. These seem to have been based on drawings Hollar made in Holland in 1634, and indeed they were aimed at the Dutch market, being published in Amsterdam by Clement de Jonghe, Rem-

brandt's friend and sitter. The work of a well-established school of Dutch marine artists was echoed in a tradition of prints that goes back to Brueghel and Frans Huys and includes the crisp views of river shipping in prints by Jan van de Velde. Some of Hollar's ships, wallowing in heavy seas or careening along in a fresh breeze, have counterparts in contemporary Dutch prints. Yet his original contribution lay in formalized compositions of ships standing in harbor and swarming with dockyard workers. Two prints of Dutch West Indiamen (no. 81) are outright masterpieces, lyrical tributes to the charms of masts, rigging, bowsprits, and carved bulkheads—seen in close-up, dramatically edited by the confining lines of the border. A flagpole positions itself neatly between the letters of the inscription, a seaman climbs the rigging to the top of the design like a spider in a web, the jutting bowsprit has a bold assurance of motion in a design that resolves with great simplicity the motions of complex shapes. This is not the salty world of Willem van de Velde or Porcellis, with their choppy waves and billowing sails; it is more akin, albeit humbler, to the poetry of geometry in Seurat's paintings at Gravelines.[70]

SECOND ENGLISH PERIOD

Hollar returned in 1652 to a changed London, Aubrey records. "When he first came to England (which was a serene time of peace) . . . the people, both poore and rich, did looke cheerfully, but at his returne, he found the countenances of the people all changed, melancholy, spightfull, as if bewitched."[71] While in Antwerp Hollar converted to Catholicism, which caused him problems in London. In 1656 he was arrested for worshipping at a banned Catholic service.

The glum Puritan England to which he returned would seem to have held scant attraction for Hollar, considering the abundance of varied work that he was finding in Antwerp. There may have been family reasons for returning; his wife, after all, was English. Moreover, Parliament had offered exiled royalists an olive branch in the shape of the 1652 Act of Pardon and Oblivion, which occasioned the return of many wandering royalists. Additionally, the prosperity of Antwerp had been undermined by the terms of the 1646 Treaty of Munster, which demanded the closure of the Schelde, on which the city's wealth depended. London was to remain his home for the rest of his life. They were years marked by unstinting, often uncongenial labor, personal hardship and grief, and professional disappointment, occasioned by the catastrophes visited upon London. The days of the costume sets, muffs, and subjects engendered by a spirit of wealth and seduction were now over, and the whole character of his work became more functional and austere.

King Charles I was beheaded in 1649, an event noted by Hollar in Antwerp with a delicate valedictory portrait (no. 79), and his great collection of pictures was dispersed at auction by the Commonwealth. Van Dyck's preeminence as a portraitist had been inherited by Sir Peter Lely, who lived in state in Covent Garden and from whom Hollar could expect as little in the way of patronage as he had from Van Dyck. Samuel Cooper was at the height of his powers as a miniaturist, and his reputation for catching a likeness must have thrown Hollar's shortcomings in that respect into sharper relief.[72] In the Bohemian's absence England had failed to produce any native etchers of note, but Faithorne had spent a period of exile in Paris, where he had learned to refine his manner, and from his return in 1650 he monopolized the best commissions for portrait prints.

Hollar's future lay mainly with the booksellers and publishers, notably John Ogilby and William Dugdale, and his name is inseparable from their ambitious ventures. Some of these projects kept him engaged for months at a time. Ogilby was one of the most energetic and self-promoting men of the Stuart period.[73] The son of a Scottish debtor, Ogilby was first a dancer; he then became a dancing master and man of the theater. In that capacity he founded, managed, and directed Dublin's first theater. These were poor qualifications for life in Cromwell's England, and at midlife he changed careers, learning Greek and Latin and setting up as a translator and publisher. He was among the first in England to issue large folio volumes that were packed with engraved plates and subsidized by the dedicatees of each plate, who paid handsomely to see their names writ large in such prestigious volumes. Ogilby's fame is deserved, but the availability and industry of Hollar is the central pillar on which it rests. His folio *Virgil* was published in 1654. Hollar began working on the forty-four etchings for the book in 1652, but only his technical skills were required because he was copying drawings by Frans Clein. In some plates the labor was divided; for example, *Aeneas and the Golden Bough* (no. 103) reveals Hollar's hand in the etched landscape, but the figure is clearly engraved, probably by William Faithorne. This plate was subsidized at the usual cost of £10 by Elias Ashmole.

A more sympathetic congenial commission from Ogilby

was *The Entertainment of Charles II in his Passage Through the City of London* (1662; no. 107). Although the trotting figures of the procession have a somewhat crunched-up appearance, the scenes are never without animation, and Hollar excelled in depicting the Lilliputian but self-congratulatory host in Westminster Abbey at the coronation. Hollar again relied on Clein's drawings for the plates to Ogilby's large and luxurious *Fables of Aesop* of 1665, which was reissued with additional plates and additional fables by Ogilby himself in 1668. Only occasionally do these sparkle, as when some theme touched a chord with Hollar's own private interests, such as that in *The Swan and the Stork* (fig. 15). That print reminds us how much we missed by Hollar's exclusion from the spectator stalls of the fashionable world.

Hollar's only English rival as an etcher was the engaging figure of Francis Barlow, who was probably inviting direct

15. Wenceslaus Hollar. *The Swan and the Stork*. Etching. From Ogilby's *Aesopics*. British Museum, London.

16. Francis Barlow. *The Cock and Precious Stone.* Pen and brown ink. From *Aesop's Fables.* British Museum, London.

comparison when he published, in 1666, an edition of Aesop's fables with 110 small etched plates (fig. 16).[74] His "Apologia" states that he was no "professed Graver or Eacher, but a Well-Wisher to the Art of Painting; and therefore Designe is all we aim at, and cannot perform Curious Neatness without losing the Spirit, which is the main." The breezy gusto and improvisation of Barlow's etchings is in marked contrast with Hollar's careful manner, and it seems likely that Barlow's words constitute a friendly broadside at the older artist's habitual neatness. Even Hollar's most blinkered admirers must admit that Barlow's barnyard baroque, with rapid wiry lines dashing out clucking fowl and cunning foxes, is a welcome contrast to the sedate lines of the Bohemian. Hollar's approach to the animal kingdom was essentially a static one, attuned to description of plumage or to the fur of a dead mole (no. 89). Barlow's approach is more that of the huntsman, based on motion and on an understanding of animals' natural habitat. Barlow's other etchings include some unsigned plates for a strange poem by Edward Benlowes called "Theophila" (1652), and a number of separate plates, including satires, from different periods of his career. Ultimately he became a collaborator with Hollar, who etched his drawings for *Severall Wayes of Hunting, Hawking, and Fishing According to the English Manner* (1671). Hollar also etched Barlow's elaborate and rollicking title page to Ogilby's *Britannia* (1675).

Hollar's arrival in England sparked an interest in etching, which was deemed a suitable activity even for an educated amateur. John Evelyn, a friend and admirer of Hollar, seems to have been the first Englishman to etch his own designs, publishing sets of landscapes in 1649.[75] Although they lack the sophistication of his drawing *Italian Landscape* (no. 114), they stand at the beginning of a notable native tradition of amateur etchers. Evelyn was also the first Englishman to write about prints; indeed, his book *Sculptura* is the first history of prints in any language, and one where Hollar's work is mentioned with approbation. It was naturally to Hollar that Evelyn turned when he designed the frontispiece to Thomas Sprat's *The History of the Royal Society* in 1667, the professional presumably refining and improving the drawing of the amateur.

A number of minor etchers are loosely associated with Hollar, though none appears to have been a pupil. Richard Gaywood (fl.1650–1680), Thomas Dudley (fl.1678), Edmund Marmion (fl.1656), and Peregrine Lovell (fl.1670's) all made etchings and sometimes copied Hollar, but they are feeble artists who add little to our knowledge of the period. Only Francis Place, a gentleman amateur and a friend of Hollar but by his own statement to Vertue "never his pupil, which was my misfortune," benefited from Hollar's help and acted as a conduit for his influence on later generations. As an etcher Place cut his teeth on Leonardesque caricatures before graduating to landscape. He even essayed the new technique of mezzotint in a gentle portrait of his friend William Lodge (no. 121). His landscape drawings often adopt a Hollaresque panoramic format but are frequently more suggestive of atmosphere and less concerned with amplitude of line (nos. 116–119).[76]

Perhaps the most regrettable loss among the many lost drawings by Hollar is the watercolor of Stonehenge recorded by Vertue in the collection of Lord Burlington. Hollar's second period in England is strongly associated with the new spirit of antiquarianism, touchingly evoked in Barlow's little drawing of two peasants gazing with wonder at a megalithic monument (no. 113). John Aubrey, whose notes on Hollar constitute the most important and personal contemporary source on the artist's life, was from his earliest years a passionate antiquarian (fig. 17). His notes are permeated with the grief he felt, even as a schoolboy, at the casual way that his father's generation destroyed ancient monuments and antiquities. While hunting at Christmastime in 1648, he rode through the village of Avebury where he was "wonderfully surprised at the sight of those vast stones, of which I had never heard before."[77] Utterly unregarded, the stones were even then being destroyed by the villagers to build cottages, and without his records we would have scant idea of the magnitude of these great stone circles, in comparison with which Stonehenge is but a dainty chaplet of stone. Medieval relics were equally at risk as the zealous Puritans turned random destruction into controlled and ordered demolition. The stained glass in churches the length and breadth of England was smashed, and monuments and statues were pulverized. Aubrey was not alone in realizing the importance of recording what was left of England's past, and for these earnest antiquarians the art of Hollar was a vital tool.

William Dugdale and Ogilby were Hollar's main employers in London (fig. 18). Dugdale's books were almost entirely anti-

17. William Faithorne. *John Aubrey*. Crayon and colored chalk. Ashmolean Museum, Oxford.

18. Wenceslaus Hollar. *William Dugdale*. Etching. Frontispiece to *The Antiquities of Warwickshire*. British Museum, London.

quarian in spirit, and Hollar's contributions to them began as soon as he had completed work on Ogilby's *Virgil*. He made numerous etchings for Dugdale's *Monasticon Anglicanum* (1655), *Antiquities of Warwickshire* (1658) and, most important, *History of St. Paul's* (1658). Dugdale had been among the first to sense the impending danger to ancient English structures, and as early as 1641 he had, with admirable prescience, commissioned drawings of monuments in London churches. Dugdale's histories were based on dedicated research into genealogies, rolls, charters, and registers, and such papers writhe and flutter in the background of Hollar's portrait of Dugdale. Hollar's prints were intended to add flesh to those bare bones. In fact, Hollar's success in the epic volumes of *Monasticon* varied. Frequently he was working from drawings supplied to him; in other cases his interest flagged. *Salisbury*

Cathedral is a success, *Lincoln Cathedral* a failure (fig. 19). Often the sound of the treadmill is not far away, and Hollar's lines are ground into regimentation and dryly printed. Dugdale seems to have directed the artist to work within certain guidelines, the first of which must have been, "Don't include too many figures to distract attention from the buildings." *Lincoln* has a bedraggled trio of figures and *Salisbury* several groups, but poor *Lichfield* has not a single verger lurking in the shadows. The buildings and monuments are all. These etchings, when compared with those of Antwerp and Strasbourg cathedrals, have a disheartening lack of animation and verisimilitude.

Dugdale's *History of St. Paul's Cathedral* appeared in 1658, and even the pessimistic Dugdale could not have foreseen its destruction in the Great Fire. The unloved old hybrid of

19. Wenceslaus Hollar. *Lincoln Cathedral*. Etching. From *Monasticon Anglicanum*. British Museum, London.

crumbling Gothic enhanced by Inigo Jones's Corinthian West Front is thus preserved only in Hollar's plates. Both interior and exterior views are devoid of figures, and perhaps Dugdale intended this as a censorious statement. He swept away the tradesmen, strollers, and buskers who had for years thronged the building, converting it from a place of worship into a sordid common thoroughfare. The etching of much of the detail is fine, and the perspective of the Norman nave marvelous, but many of the plates are parched and desiccated in feeling. Moreover, in certain plates, such as *Crypt*, Hollar has laid his lines too close, so that in the hurried printing there are piebald areas where the lines have failed to take the ink. Fine proof impressions, which are carefully printed and aside from the book, seem not to have been available. Dugdale's patronage was enlightened, generous, and percipient, and it gave the artist employment when it was most needed. But employment it was; the artist was not untrammeled, and, sadly, his work lacks the airy spirit and contentment of his early work.

The third volume of *Monasticon*, with thirty plates by Hollar, was published in 1673. In the previous year appeared Elias Ashmole's *The Institution, Laws and Ceremonies of the Most Noble Order of the Garter*, with fifty etchings by Hollar. He had been working on these plates since 1660, and even before that Ashmole recorded visits to Windsor with Hollar to make sketches on the spot. There is a lightheartedness about this work that distinguishes it from the Dugdale work. Hollar had always enjoyed working at Windsor, and the project was far more leisurely than other commissions of the period. The bird's-eye *View of Windsor* is among his most assured essays in this mode, and the gentle serpentine *Grand Procession of the Soveraigne and Knightly Companions* is at once a display of Restoration luxury and a delightful contrast to the swaggering hauteur of Lely's great drawings of the knights in procession.

Hollar's labors were not all devoted to Dugdale, Ogilby, and Ashmole. There are scores of portraits, maps, and illustrations, as well as such enchanting personal ventures as the *Views Near London* (no. 100). The artist's indefatigable industry is legendary. Place informed Vertue that "he did all by the hour in which he was very exact for if anybody came in that kept him from his business he always laid ye hour glass on one side, till they were gone. he always rcev'd 12 pence an hour."[78] Hollar's most ambitious personal project of these years, and the one that surely was closest to his heart, can be categorized by Hollar students only as the "Tragedy of the

Map." In 1660 he issued an etched flysheet, a prospectus that is of such importance that it is here printed in full:

> *Propositions Concerning the Map of* LONDON *and Westminster etc; which is in hand by Wentzel Hollar. This Map is to contain 10 Foot in bredth, and 5 Foot upward wherein shall be expressed, not onely the Streets, Lanes, Alleys, etc: proportionally measured; but also the Buildings (especially of the principal Houses, Churches, Courts, Halls; etc) as much resembling the likeness of them, as the Convenience of the roome will permit. Example whereof is in considerable part to be seen; the Charge thereof being found by Experience to be very great and too heavy to be borne by the Author himselve alone, He makes this proposall following. If any Gentleman or other Worthy Person be inclined to encouradge arts, or things of that nature, would please (out of his free benevolence and Generous mind, not standing upon Profit, but for the Honour of this famous Cittie, and his owne) to contribute to this laborious Peece, the summe of 3lb, in a maner as shall follow: he will thereby be obliged, in way of gratuity, to put every such persons Coat of Armes and Name as a Benefactour, in a Convenient place of the Map designed for that purpose. And the Worke being finished, to deliuer to each of them 2 such Maps printed, full and Compleat. The maner of the payment is desired to be thus; 20 Shil now to help on the Worke, and to support & maintaine the Charges which doe occur, as well in his Family or otherwise, and at the sight of their Coats of Armes in their places, 20 Shil moore, and at the receit of their Compleate maps the last mony is to be payd.*[79]

It would appear that this prospectus was accompanied by a specimen—"example whereof is in considerable part to be seen"—and it is possible that this is to be identified with the beautiful bird's-eye view *West Central Area of London* (no. 102). The only preserved impression of that view is in the British Museum. Certainly this shows a large enough part of London to qualify as "considerable." If this identification is accepted, then the map that we see is evidently on a reduced scale from that which was planned—in other words, viewed from higher up. The bird's-eye view of the finished large map would have been lower, allowing detailed representation of individual houses.[80]

Hollar's project was intended to be his masterpiece—a map that would transcend all others in scale and detail, a task of vaulting ambition for which he alone was qualified by experience and accumulated material. Hollar was accustomed to drawing from high spots, but his experience was only partial preparation for this project, as in bird's-eye views the buildings are seen from a much higher perspective. The tradition of such engraved views goes back to Renaissance editions of the world maps of Ptolemy. Jacobo Barbari's woodcut of Venice stands as the *ne plus ultra* of the art. Such views were also common in Netherlandish printmaking, the tradition which Hollar, through his tutelage with Merian, enhanced by such works as his views of Düren, Hull, and Oxford. His view of London is one of the most beautiful of all, by reason not merely of its detail and execution but also of a certain gravitas in its presentation and design. Yet it is a tragedy that we are left, in effect, with only the overture to the main event.[81]

The Great Fire of 1666 consigned his project to oblivion. Hollar survived the terrible plague of 1665, though his son James—according to Aubrey, "an ingeniose youth, drew delicately"—succumbed. The fire was a fresh tribulation for the unfortunate artist. A general conflagration was not entirely unexpected; as recently as 1665 Charles II had written to the Lord Mayor, expressing his fear that a fire could break out in the crowded London streets, with their overhanging medieval wooden houses. Hysterical prophets, in which the age abounded, had also screamed their warnings. Walter Costello sounded a grim warning in his treatise of 1658: "London, go on still in thy presumptious wickedness! put the end day far from thee, and repent not! do so London. But if fire make not ashes of the city, and thy bones also, conclude me a liar for ever. Oh, London! London! sinful as Sodom and Gomorrah! the decree is gone out, repent, or burn, as Sodom, as Gomorrah!"[82]

The fire began in a baker's kitchen in Pudding Lane, near London Bridge. It started slowly, and such observers as Samuel Pepys initially had little fear, nor indeed much curiosity, since fires were a common occurrence.[83] Succored by helpful winds, however, the fires raged for four days, destroying a vast swath of London, including St. Paul's Cathedral. It has been assumed by some commentators that Hollar was able to sketch the city as it burned, but this is most unlikely. He was in fact in great danger—not from the flames, which claimed only one or two victims, but from rampaging mobs of xenophobic Londoners, egged on by ferocious harridans, who believed that the fire was the handiwork of foreigners. The wind blew blazing fragments ahead of the course of the fire, creating sudden blazes in places previously unaffected. This gave the impression that foreign agents were roaming the city, hurling firebombs into houses. Anyone who spoke broken English was in danger. A Frenchman in Moorfields was attacked and practically dismembered for carrying "balls of fire" in a chest. They were later found to be tennis balls. It is likely that Hollar was in hiding or under the protection of friends, venturing forth only when the flames had died.

At St. Paul's the destruction wreaked a tragedy within a tragedy. Scores of booksellers who worked around the churchyard had moved their stock into the crypt of the cathedral, believing it to be fireproof. It was not, and charred fragments of paper fluttered down for miles around. Dugdale lamented that "nearly three-hundred of my books of Paul's [cathedral] and about 500 of my History of Embanking and Draining, perished also in these flames, and what troubles me not the least—my whole copy, except thirty sheets which were printed, of the third volume of the *Monasticon Anglicanum*, through the great negligence of my printer."[84] It would be a sad irony indeed if Dugdale's stock of "Paul's" was consumed in the destruction of the very building it recorded.

John Ogilby's printing house in King's Head Court, Shoe Lane, was also burned out, yet even Walter Bell—the sober historian of the Great Fire—cannot conceal his merriment at the loss of Ogilby's *Carolies,* an epic poem in twelve books written in honor of Charles I—"the pride, divertisement, business and sole comfort of my age."[85] Vertue records that at the time of the plague Hollar was living in Bloomsbury. If he was still there at the time of the Great Fire he would have been safe, since the flames did not reach that far.

Hollar's skills were immediately in demand in the aftermath of this disaster as Londoners took stock of the devastation and began to plan their new city. Hollar repaired to the steeple of St. Mary Overy in Southwark to observe from south of the river and make the panoramic drawings for his *London Before and After the Great Fire* (no. 105). In other plates he maps the devastated area and the appearance of the city in flames. Yet the profit from these plates was offset by the increasingly dim prospects for his Great Map, for the currency of a map showing a city largely destroyed was much diminished. In October 1666 Hollar petitioned the king for the official status of His Majesty's Scenographer, hoping that the post would help him finance and complete his Great View, which had already left him greatly out of pocket (see appendix 1). Samuel Pepys entered in his diary on 22 November 1666 that "my Lord Bruncker did show me Hollar's new print of the City, with a pretty representation of that part which is burnt, very fine indeed; and tells me that the King commanded him to go on with his Great Map of the City—which he was upon before the City was burned, like Gombout [*sic*] of Paris, which I am glad of."[86]

Hollar petitioned the king again in August 1667, asking with increasing desperation for money to complete "his monument and masterpiece" to which he had devoted seven years' work and gone £100 into debt. "And now the city being destroyed," he wrote, "no man living can leave such a record to posterity—of how it was as himself."[87] All of this was to no avail; Hollar's masterpiece was not to be. Yet it is possible that a tarnished echo of his work can be found in the so-called Ogilby and Morgan *Large Map of London,* published by Ogilby in 1677 with a dedication to Charles II. This was the year of Hollar's death, but there is no mention of his name on any of the twenty large plates that make up the map. Pennington finds Hollar's hand in much of the etched work, while Hind believed that the plan owed much to Hollar, but the execution little.[88] It seems likely therefore that the self-serving Ogilby took advantage of Hollar's death by quickly issuing a bastardized version of his unfinished work. But to glimpse his high designs the student should spurn Ogilby's product for Hollar's *West Central Area of London,* a loving homage to his adopted city.

Hollar's seeming abandonment of the Great Map and his urgent need for new and profitable employment are evidenced by his journey to Tangier in 1669, the final great event of his life. The history of the colony at Tangier is one of the less glorious episodes in Britain's imperial history.[89] This gloomy habitation in Morocco, directly across the strait from Gibraltar, had been part of the dowry of Catherine of Braganza when she married Charles II in 1662. It consisted of an isolated, elaborately constructed fort, and the various towers and fortifications bore such homely English names as Norwood and Whitby. It was constantly attacked and difficult to defend, and by 1669 it was proving a drain on the nation's purse, not the hoped for source of profit. In 1669 Lord Henry Howard was sent out on an embassy to report on its viability.

Howard was the grandson of Arundel, and Hollar used this family connection to underpin yet another petition to the king in March 1669. He asked to be attached to Howard's embassy as "Scenographer to His Majesty" for the purpose of making accurate topographical drawings of the settlement (appendix 1). For this arduous task he asked for "one Hundred pounds towards the fitting of my selve and leaving my House and Family in good condition in my absence."[90]

During his residence in Tangier, Hollar made numerous panoramic views, of which about thirty survive.[91] They include a number of large and highly finished watercolors that are painted in cool tints of green and blue and enlivened by the sealing-wax reds of the soldiers' coats. They are among his grandest works, and the rolling, undulating lines that track the contours of the hills are reminiscent of the panoramic view of Greenwich. Their purpose is topographic, but the platoons of soldiers marching dejectedly or lounging by their cannon also give Hollar an unacknowledged status as Britain's first war artist. Both the drawings and the set of prints he made on his return to England suggest the sheer ennui and boredom of garrison life in a remote country. The tradition of honestly chronicling the vicissitudes of military life has continued to the twentieth century in the watercolors of such artists as Edward Bawden, Eric Ravilious, and Edward Ardizzone. The embassy failed in its purpose—indeed, Hollar seems to have been something of an albatross to official embassies—and as the party returned to England in December 1669 it was unsuccessfully attacked by Turkish pirates.[92] Hollar was not to leave England again.

The scraps of information that have come down to us are not enough to reconstruct a picture of the artist's social circle or of the intellectual ambience in which he lived. Sheer toil must have limited his social life, and his abstemious habits would have restricted his intimacy with the likes of John Aubrey. John Evelyn seems to have been genuinely fond of the artist, as was Sir Edward Walker. Hollar's work reflects the tremendous intellectual vitality of Stuart London, its boundless curiosity and hunger for knowledge of every kind, yet Hollar was not an intellectual nor a speculative artist. Rather, his work is the tool by which the curiosity of others could be illustrated. Evelyn keenly regretted that he did not possess Hollar's work "entire," and the encyclopedic nature of his oeuvre had by the early eighteenth century, and probably before, attracted collectors eager to purchase every print, which they would paste into albums.

The London intellectual world of poetry, science, and philosophy, to which the artist was a quiet bystander, was one of marvelous and strident energy that also found expression in colonial expansion. This is the world of the Royal Society, of Robert Hooke, John Evelyn, and Thomas Hobbes. Hooke, the physicist, mathematician, and inventor—scuttling from meeting to meeting, his head buzzing with ideas—was as comfortable with an architect's drawing board as with a microscope, which he had perfected (no. 112). Sir Christopher Wren, who was rebuilding the city yet was still concerned with new techniques of printmaking, looms large in the pages of Hooke's extraordinary diary.[93] Royal personages were not mere spectators; Prince Rupert presented to the English public his achievements in mezzotint (no. 115), a seductive medium that may have made Hollar's style seem old-fashioned.[94] In many poems and essays we find an increasing delight in nature, in the natural phenomena of the world, those manifestations of creation to be seen on every side. To all these enthusiasms, Hollar had contributed his part, by quietly creating the viable means by which they could be noted and circulated abroad.

Hollar died in 1677. Aubrey recorded that he "dyed poor" but later altered this to "dyed not riche." The inventory of his possessions drawn up after his death and rediscovered by Robert Harding is evidence of his humble circumstances (see appendix 2). His old age cannot have been anything but wearisome and disillusioned, the congenial employment of his years with Arundel but a fading memory. England was greatly in his debt, not merely for his recording so many lost buildings, so many evanescent ruffs, muffs, and silken dresses, but for single-handedly establishing a tradition of etching and a long and fruitful history of topographical art. He created a few great prints and many good ones, yet it is the gentle modesty of his work, the affectionate curvature of his delicate etched lines, that has assured him a lasting place in our affections.

Appendix 1

In October 1666 Hollar wrote to the King to ask for the official status of His Majesty's Scenographer. His letter follows:

To his most Excellent Majestie, Charles the Second
King of England:
Humble Petition of Wenceslaus Hollar.
Sheweth That: Whereas your Majestie had many Yeares since a sufficient knowledge of my abilities in designing of prospects Landskips, Citties, Castles & other things of that Nature.

My humble Request is; That your Majestie be pleased to bestow upon me the Honour & Tittle of your Majesties Scenographer; or designer of Prospects aforesaid, with a Priviledge that no Person in your Majs Dominions may meddle to Copie or Cause to be Copied directly or indirectly any such things as I might produce, by my owne Study witt or Industry.

And if your Majestie would please, to give me some Encouragement, as would forward the finishing of my Map of London (whereof your Majest: had seene some part) that my paines already taken besides Expenses might not be utterlie lost, it will doubtless induce others to doe the like, and to becom Benefactors, & the Worke beeing perfected it will prove a very remarkable Monument & record to all posteritie And I shall ever pray for your Majest; prosperous Rayne.

31 Oct. 66
That he may be his Maties Sole Scenographer and . . . have supplies for ye. finishing his map of London.
Public Record Office 110, 125

Appendix 2

According to Francis Place, in his letter to George Vertue, Hollar's financial distress in his last days was so great that, as he lay dying, the bailiffs were actually in the house seizing his goods. The feeble artist asked them pathetically to leave him his bed to die in. The recent discovery by Robert Harding of the inventory of his possessions drawn up after his death is a partial corrective to this legend. It is not known how much he was in debt, but his sudden death of an "Apoplextick fitt" would have thwarted the bailiffs.

It was known that Hollar died, intestate, on 25 March 1677 at his house in Gardiner's Lane, Westminster (no longer in existence), and that administration of his estate was granted to his second wife, Honora, on 25 May 1677 (Commissary Court of Westminster, Act Book 1667–1679, f.121b: Westminster City Archives Acc. 120/6). An inventory of his possessions, which were valued at £22, was known to have been taken, but until now was presumed lost. It is here published for the first time.

The inventory was listed in the *Calender of Grants of Probate and Administration . . . . of the Commisary Court of . . . Westminster* (London, 1864) 253, and in A. M. Burke, *Indexes to the Ancient Testamentary Records of Westminster* (London, 1913) 40 (Inv. vi. 298). The probate records were transferred from Westminster Abbey to the Principal Probate Registry in the early 1860s, and the Hollar inventory was mentioned in the 1864 list; in 1913 Burke noted that the remaining inventories were arranged there in bundles. The inventories, however, were not transferred with the wills to the city of Westminster Archives and seem to have passed via St. Paul's Cathedral and the Guildhall Library in the city of London (an unlikely resting place for documents pertaining to a resident of Westminster), before being returned to Westminster Abbey in 1981, where they now make up muniment A 1/6 (1677).

The inventory shows that, with £22 of goods and chattels, Hollar and his family lived in relative if somewhat shabby comfort for the time, though a light-year away from the grand establishment of a successful artist like Sir Peter Lely. It is difficult to transcribe £22 into a modern sum, but it may be observed that when Hollar went to Tangier he asked the king for £100 for "the fitting of my selve and leaving my House and Family in good condition." Furthermore, for a single plate of Dugdale's *St. Paul's* volume Hollar received £5 with Dugdale writing "Mr. Hollar, who is to receive

the 5 l for the Lord Darcye's plate." By any middle-class standards, £22 was not a lot, and the family dined off pewter plates, not china.

Hollar rented a house seemingly of three stories plus a furnished garret—a room that did not then have the pitiful domestic connotations that it would acquire in the eighteenth century. The inventory, as is usual for the time, pays particular attention to the three beds and the fabrics ("the greene Baze Curtains & vallance" and the "hangins of old striped stuffe"). It is possible that the room containing the three tables, the "Skreetore" (presumably an escritoire—a writing table), a trunk, and two stools was Hollar's workroom. If the house was of three storeys, this would have been its largest room, occupying the first floor (or second floor, according to American usage).

No doubt the inventory was hurriedly drawn up, but certain items are still conspicuous by their absence. A printing press is a large and valuable item, and it could not possibly have been omitted. So it must be assumed that at his death Hollar had no printing or proofing facilities in his house. Also unmentioned are other expensive items, such as books, paper, acid, and etching tools. There is no reference to drawings, which surely existed in abundance, unless they were lumped in with the prints. Nor is there any mention of copper plates, the most valuable commodity of all to the artist's widow. Many had

been sold years before, of course, and much of Hollar's work in his second English period had been for book publishers, who would have owned the plates. But even so one would expect some residue to have survived. The fittings of the house were utilitarian; Hollar seems not to have had a single picture or map hanging on the walls. He owned two rugs and a carpet, and it is reasonable to surmise that they were threadbare.

The final item of "prints belonging to the decds: trade" is the most intriguing, but it is also the most frustrating in the brevity of its description. Was this Hollar's own collection of his prints, possibly the "volume" of prints that Vertue informs us was purchased from Honora Hollar by Sir Hans Sloane and subsequently given to the British Museum? Our knowledge of Hollar strongly suggests that he was a compulsive hoarder of his own work, especially drawings, which he frequently used later for prints. It is quite likely that his own collection of work—his widow's principal inheritance—was not listed at all on the inventory and was accounted for separately. The manuscript catalogue of Sir Hans Sloane's Library notes "a large volume pasted full of copper cuts, all etched by Mr. Wenceslaus Hollar," and added in a later hand is the information that these were "his own proof prints, bought of his widow, and with an index by Dr. Scheuchzer." (Scheuchzer died in 1729.) Did other such volumes exist?

An Inventory of all the Goods & of all the goods chattles & Houshold stuff of Wincislaues Holler late of the Parish of St. Margarets in the Citty of Westminster decds taken & apprized the 6th day of April in the yeare of our Lord 1677 by Edward Lingly the true tenner of wch: Inventory is as followeth viz:

Imprimis in the garret one bedstead, 1 bed
   and boulster
   one table too stooles

In the chamber belowe one bedstead
   A bed and boulster 2 blanketts & one Rugg
   one table one screene and one chest one
   [trunk ?]

Item in the next chamber one Bedstead
   bed & Boylster, 2 blanketts one Rugg
   & the grene Baze Curtaines & vallance
   4 Chairs one Tble & Carpet one lookeing
   glasse & Andyrons

Item in the chamber belowe 3 Tables
   one skreetore one Truncke & 2 stooles

Item in the parlour 4 cheares one
   table one chest of drauers and the
   hangins of old striped stuffe

Item in the Kitchin one Jack 3 spits
   1 warming pan & A dripinpan 1 gridyron
   4 chears 1 table A brass kettle 2 bras
   pots 2 kettels & 10 peeces of peueter

Item prints belonging to the decds:
trade- - - - - - - - - - - - - - - - - - -

All these goods were valued to the
summe of - - - - - - - - - - - - - - - - - XX11 li.
Extim fait [?] 250 Maij
1677 per [..]

Notes

1. John Aubrey, *Aubrey's Brief Lives*, ed. Oliver Lawson Dick (London, 1949), 324–325.

2. See Craig Hartley, "The Young Hollar in Prague: A Group of New Acquisitions," *Print Quarterly* 8 (September 1991): plate 148.

3. See Richard Godfrey, "Hollar's Last View of Prague," *Print Quarterly* 9 (September 1992): 288–290, plate 151.

4. See Hartley, "Young Hollar in Prague," 252–274. See also Vladimir Denkstein, *Hollar Drawings* (London, 1979); and J. I. Pav, "Wenceslaus Hollar in Germany 1627–1636," *Art Bulletin* 55 (January 1973).

5. Aubrey, *Aubrey's Brief Lives*, 324–325. See John Evelyn, *The Diary of John Evelyn*, ed. E. S. de Beer (Oxford, 1955), 1: 21–22. A note was added at a later date to his entry for 23 May 1641.

6. Denkstein, *Hollar Drawings*.

7. For an excellent and well-illustrated survey see Thomas DaCosta Kaufmann, *The School of Prague: Painting at the Court of Rudolf II* (Chicago, 1988). See also *Prag um 1600* (Kulturstiftung Ruhr Essen, 1988).

8. See Timothy Riggs and Larry Silver, *Graven Images: The Rise of Professional Printmaking in Antwerp and Haarlem 1540–1640* (Chicago: Northwestern University Press, 1993). See also *The Stylish Image: Printmakers of the Court of Rudolf II*, introduction by R. J. W. Evans and Eliska Fucikova, with catalogue notes by Mungo Campbell (Edinburgh: National Gallery of Scotland, 1991).

9. Lars Olof Larsson, *Adrian de Vries: Adrianus Fries Hagiensis Batavus 1545–1626* (Vienna, 1967).

10. See Lee Hendrix and Thea Vignau-Wilberg, *Mira Calligraphiae Monumenta: A Sixteenth-Century Calligraphic Manuscript* (Malibu, Calif.: J. Paul Getty Museum, 1992).

11. See F. W. H. Hollstein, *Dutch and Flemish Etchings, Engravings and Woodcuts*, vols. 21 and 22 (Amsterdam, 1980), ed. Karel G. Boon.

12. Hollstein, vol. 38 (Roosendaal, 1991), ed. D. De Hop Scheffer, comp. Christiaan Schuckman.

13. Aubrey, *Aubrey's Brief Lives*, 324–325.

14. Hartley, "Young Hollar in Prague."

15. Hollstein, vol. 1, no. 143 (Amsterdam, 1954).

16. Denkstein, *Hollar Drawings*, plate 12. Adam Elsheimer also made a drawing of Fortune for a Friendship Album; see Keith Andrews, *Adam Elsheimer* (Munich, 1985), plate 11, no. 27.

17. For a catalogue of the drawings see Franz Sprinzels [Francis Springell], *Hollar Handzeichnungen* (Vienna, 1938). This is a somewhat unwieldy tool, and the small reproductions are of modest value. The author changed his name when he moved to England after the German occupation of Czechoslovakia.

18. See David Freedberg, *Dutch Landscape Prints of the Seventeenth Century* (London: British Museum, 1988), 28–32.

19. Denkstein, *Hollar Drawings*, plates 2–3.

20. For a copiously illustrated survey of the Cologne years see *Wenzel Hollar. Die Kolner Jahre: Zeichnungen und Radierung, 1632–1636* (Cologne, 1992).

21. See Lucas Heinrich Wuthrich, *Das Druckgraphische Werk von Matthaeus Merina D. Ae*, 2 vols. (Basel, 1972).

22. See Gary Scwartz, *Rembrandt: His Life, His Paintings* (London, 1985), 289.

23. For an exhaustive and well-illustrated study of Hollar's works associated with the Rhine see *Wenzel Hollar: Reisebilder vom Rhein* (Mainz: Landesmuseum, 1985–1987).

24. For a full account of the embassy see Francis Springell, *Connoisseur and Diplomat: The Earl of Arundel's Embassy to Germany in 1636 as Recounted in William Crowne's Diary, the Earl's Letters and Other Contemporary Sources with a Catalogue of the Topographical Drawings Made on the Journey by Wenceslaus Hollar* (London, 1963). Arundel's letter to Petty is published in Mary Hervey, *The Life, Correspondence, and Collections of Thomas Howard, Earl of Arundel* (Cambridge, 1921), 365–367.

25. William Crowne, *A True Relation of All the Remarkable Places and Passages Observed in the Travels of . . . Thomas Lord Howard, Earle of Arundell . . . Ambassadour Extraordinary to his Majesty Ferdinando the Second, Emperour of Germanie, Anno Domini 1636* (London, 1637). See Springell, *Connoisseur and Diplomat*, 54–94.

26. Aubrey, *Aubrey's Brief Lives*, 324–325.

27. Ibid., 286, 292. See also Geoffrey Keynes, *The Personality of William Harvey* (Cambridge, 1949). An unsigned etching that appears to represent Harvey in old age is in the British Museum; see F. O'Donoghue, *Catalogue of Engraved British Portraits* (London: British Museum, 1910), 460. It has been variously attributed to Hollar and to Richard Gaywood. The hands and body are awkward, but the face is very fine, and an attribution to Hollar should not be precluded. O'Donoghue assumes that the print is a copy of a painting in the National Portrait Gallery, but the reverse is actually the case.

28. A blood-curdling account of Germany at this period appears in Dr. P. Vincent, *The Lamentation of Germany. Wherein, As in Glasse, We May Behold Her Miserable Condition, and Reade the Woefull Effects of Sinne* (London, 1638).

29. Hollar's fascination with crowds watching an execution is also evident in his celebrated 1641 print of the *Execution of the Earl of Strafford* (P.552).

30. The watercolor *General View of Prague from the Petrin Slope* is in the National Gallery of Prague. *The Long View* (P.880) was etched from this watercolor in 1649.

31. Springell, *Connoisseur and Diplomat*, 91.

32. Hervey, *Life, Correspondence, and Collections of Thomas Howard*, 365–366. The same letter contains Arundel's mention of Hollar's employment.

33. The Bishop of Wurzburg presented him "with one of his [the bishop's] most prized pictures, that of 'Our Lady' painted by Albrecht Dürer" (Springell, *Connoisseur and Diplomat*, 86). This picture, now lost, was not etched by Hollar.

34. Aubrey, *Aubrey's Brief Lives*, 323–324. Place's letter to George Vertue of 20 May 1716 is one of the most important sources of information about Hollar's life even though, as noted at the time by Vertue, it contains errors of fact. The second edition of Vertue's *Catalogue of Hollar's Prints* was published in 1759 with an account of Hollar's life. Place's letter is reprinted in the *Walpole Society Annual* 18 (1929–1930).

35. See David Howarth, *Lord Arundel and His Circle* (New Haven, 1985).

36. Many of the marbles are now in the Ashmolean Museum, Oxford. See *Thomas Howard, Earl of Arundel* (Oxford: Ashmolean Museum, 1986).

37. Howarth, *Lord Arundel*, 182.

38. See Kenneth Clark, *The Drawings of Leonardo da Vinci in the Collection of Her Majesty the Queen at Windsor Castle*, 2nd ed., 2 vols. (London, 1968).

39. See Peter Schatborn, *Jan Lievens, Prints and Drawings* (Amsterdam: Museum het Rembrandthuis, 1989); and Clifford Ackley, *Printmaking in the Age of Rembrandt* (Boston: Museum of Fine Arts, 1981), 142–146.

40. See Margery Corbett and Michael Norton, *Engraving in England in the Sixteenth and Seventeenth Centuries* (Cambridge: Cambridge University Press, 1964).

This catalogue is comprehensive, but it excludes Hollar and Faithorne.

41. See Louis Fagan, *A Descriptive Catalogue of the Engraved Work of William Faithorne* (London, 1988). See also A. M. Hind, "Studies in English Engraving," *Connoisseur*, August 1933.

42. Peacham is best remembered for his celebrated manual on education, *The Compleat Gentleman* (London, 1622). On Peacham's relationship with Arundel see Howarth, *Lord Arundel*, 118–121.

43. Ibid.

44. See *The Wilton Diptych* (London: National Gallery, 1993). See also Dillian Gordon, "A New Discovery in *The Wilton Diptych*," *Burlington Magazine*, October 1993, 662–667.

45. Vertue mentions an instructional drawing book by Hollar with the feathers of the Prince of Wales stamped on the cover, but this is now lost.

46. Under privilege, royal sanction was given to a print with the implicit understanding that it could not be copied without permission. See appendix 1.

47. Lucas Vorsterman was in England between 1624 and 1630.

48. See *Thomas Howard* (Oxford: Ashmolean Museum), nos. 66–67, for reproductions of *Antique Bust of a Woman* (P.590, dated 1645), and its source, the so-called "Oxford Bust." See Michael Vickers, "Hollar and the Arundel Marbles," *Country Life*, 29 March 1979, 916–917.

49. See Keith Andrews, "Elsheimer's Latona Uncovered," *Burlington Magazine*, June 1981, 350–353.

50. See, e.g., P.1610, which combines a number of Leonardo's heads and caricatures on a single oblong plate.

51. Marie Mauquoy-Hendrickx, *L'Iconographie d'Antoine Van Dyck. Catalogue Raisonné* (Brussels, 1956).

52. See Graham Reynolds, *English Portrait Miniatures* (Cambridge, 1988), 48–49.

53. Van Dyck is nowhere acknowledged on the plates, and it is to be presumed that Hollar did not wish his sources to be recognized. Sir Oliver Millar noticed Hollar's derivations in *Charles I and His Age* (London: Queen's Gallery, 1965), 32.

54. John Evelyn, *Fumifugium; Or the Inconveniences of the Aer and Smoak of London Dissipated, Together with Some Remedies* (London, 1661).

55. See *Artists and the Thames* (London: Hayward Gallery, 1979).

56. Signed and dated 1637, but most probably executed in Holland from drawings made during a sojourn in England in 1627. See John Hayes, "Claude de Jongh," *Burlington Magazine*, January 1956, 2–11.

57. Sprinzels, *Hollar Handzeichnungen*.

58. See Daphne Foskett, *Samuel Cooper* (London, 1974); and John Murdoch, Jim Murrell, Patrick J. Noon, and Roy Strong, *The English Miniature* (New Haven: Yale University Press, 1981).

59. This curious production goes through five states. The National Gallery in Prague possesses the first four. In the first state the space for the head is left blank. In the next four states the head is successively changed by different hands from James II to Henry, Duke of Gloucester, to Charles I as Prince of Wales, and finally to Charles II as a boy.

60. See Alexander Globe, *Peter Stent, London Printseller, A Catalogue Raisonné of His Engraved Prints and Books with an Historical Bibliographical Introduction* (Vancouver, 1985). This is a most valuable work, though Globe has scant sympathy for Hollar. For the most part, Stent's stock was a charnel house of bad prints, many of them reproduced by Globe.

61. See Tamsyn Williams, "Magnetic Figures: Polemical Prints of the English Revolution," in Lucy Gent and Nigel Llewellyn, eds., *Renaissance Bodies: The Human Figure in English Culture* (London, 1990), chap. 4.

62. George Vertue, "The Notebooks of George Vertue Relating to Artists and Collections in England," *Walpole Society* 18 (London, 1929), 34–35. "Hollar lived in Bloomsbury all the time of the plague, but sufferd extreamly for want of business, which Old Peter Stent made an advantage of, purchasing several of his plates for a trifle. He told me he gave him but 30 shill. for the Long View of Greenwich which very well deserd 10 or fifteen pounds." As noted by Globe, however, *Long View of Greenwich* was sold to Stent in about 1644, not during the plague, which killed Stent, as well as Hollar's son (*Peter Stent*, 33).

63. See Richard Pennington, *A Descriptive Catalogue of the Etched Work of Wenceslaus Hollar, 1607–1677* (Cambridge: Cambridge University Press, 1982), xxv; and Springell, *Connoisseur and Diplomat*, 160, n.110, translating from the original quotation in E. Dostal, *Václav Hollar* (Prague, 1924). The reference to a needle is incorrect, as Hollar would have made finishing touches with an engraver's burin.

64. An exception is *Teresa, Lady Shirley* (P.1503), after Van Dyck, of which two proofs exist; see Griffiths, nos. 122a and 122b.

65. Vertue, "Notebooks," 112; and Pennington, *Descriptive Catalogue*, xlix. Pennington mistranscribes a "half of a quarter of an hour" into "half an hour," which entirely alters the sense of Symonds' description.

66. It should be noted that in old English slang *muff* was a term for the female pudenda, and some eighteenth-century caricatures show muffs as the appurtenances of streetwalkers. It would be a mistake, however, to credit Hollar's prints with any great degree of symbolism.

67. See Sam Siegel, *A Prosperous Past: The Sumptuory Still-Life in the Netherlands* (The Hague, 1988).

68. George Vertue, *A Description of the Works of Wenceslaus Hollar* (London, 1759), 113.

69. See J. Q. Regteren Altena, *Rembrandt en Wenzel Hollar (De kronick . . . van het Rembrandthuis)* (Amsterdam, 1959), 81 ff. See also Christopher White, *Rembrandt as an Etcher* (London, 1969).

70. For Dutch maritime prints see Irene de Groot and Robert Vorstman, *Sailing Ships: Prints by Dutch Masters from the Sixteenth to the Nineteenth Century* (Amsterdam, 1980).

71. Aubrey, *Aubrey's Brief Lives*, 323–324.

72. Foskett, *Samuel Cooper*.

73. See Katherine S. Van Eerde, *John Ogilby and the Taste of His Times* (London, 1976).

74. See Edward Hodnett, *Francis Barlow: First Master of English Book Illustration* (Berkeley, Calif., 1978).

75. See Antony Griffiths, "The Etchings of John Evelyn," in David Howarth, ed., *Art and Patronage in the Caroline Courts, Essays in Honour of Sir Oliver Millar* (Cambridge, 1993). Two or three insignificant plates by Peregrine Lovell claim strict priority, but they are copies from other artists, including Hollar.

76. See Henry Hake, "Some Contemporary Records Relating to Francis Place, with a Catalogue of his Engraved Work," *Walpole Society* 10 (1922), 39–69. See also Richard Tyler, *Francis Place: An Exhibition Representing All Aspects of His Work* (York: York City Art Gallery, 1971).

77. Aubrey, *Aubrey's Brief Lives*, 50. Aubrey remarks that Charles II had been informed by Lord Brouncker that he, Aubrey, considered that Avebury "did as much excell of Stoneheng as a cathedral does a Parish

church." The king was so impressed that he command-ed Aubrey to give him and the Duke of York a guided tour of the site.

78. Vertue, "Notebooks," 112.

79. The unique copy of this flysheet is in the Folger Shakespeare Library, Washington, D.C. It was first published in Katherine S. Van Eerde, *Wenceslaus Hollar: Delineator of His Time* (Charlottesville, 1970), 69–71.

80. See Griffiths, "Etchings of John Evelyn," 63. On the basis of the specimen print, Griffiths calculates that the finished map would have covered twenty-eight sheets. This seems to me an erroneous deduction, however, for if the existing print formed only a twenty-eighth of the whole, then many of the other sheets would have shown nothing but the open country around London.

81. Pennington, *Descriptive Catalogue,* xlii.

82. Walter G. Bell, *The Great Fire of London* (London, 1920), 18.

83. Ibid., 31. It was Pepys, however, who first brought news of the fire to the court at Whitehall and was immediately given an audience with the king.

84. Ibid., 226.

85. Ibid., 227.

86. Pepys, *Diary,* 22 November 1666. Evelyn also wrote in *Sculptura* ([London, 1662], 98): "This we the more readily mention, that thereby we may stimulate and encourage the lovers of their country freely to con-tribute to the like attempt of the above mentioned Mr. Hollar, and enable him to proceed with what is now under his hand, for the honour of our imperial City." This is preceded by a reference to Gomboust's map.

87. Pennington, *Descriptive Catalogue,* xlii.

88. See A. M. Hind, *Wenceslaus Hollar and His Views of London and Windsor in the Seventeenth Century* (Lon-don, 1922), no. 6, 33–34.

89. For a history of the colony of Tangier see E. M. G. Routh, *Tangier: England's Lost Atlantic Outpost* (Lon-don, 1912). See also Francis Springell, "Unpublished Drawings of Tangier by Wenceslaus Hollar," *Burlington Magazine,* February 1964, 69–74.

90. Quoted in Pennington, *Descriptive Catalogue,* xlvi, from Public Record Office, Calendar State Paper Domicile 1668–1669, part 1, no. 40, March 1668–1669.

91. The most important group is in the British Muse-um; see Edward Croft-Murray and Paul Hulton, *Cata-logue of British Drawings,* vol. 1, *XVI & XVII Centuries* (London: British Museum, 1960).

92. Hollar made an etching depicting the engagement (P.1247).

93. See H. W. Robinson and W. Adams, eds., *The Diary of Robert Hooke* (London, 1935), which contains a num-ber of interesting references to prints and to the print trade.

94. First published in Evelyn's *Sculptura.* For an essay on Prince Rupert's prints see A. M. Hind, "Studies in English Engraving, Part VI, Prince Rupert and the Beginnings of Mezzotint," *Connoisseur,* December 1933, 388.

Plates

Plate 1. *The Wooden Gate at Düren.* Pen and brown ink over black chalk, with brown, gray, and pale green wash. 1634. (no. 5)

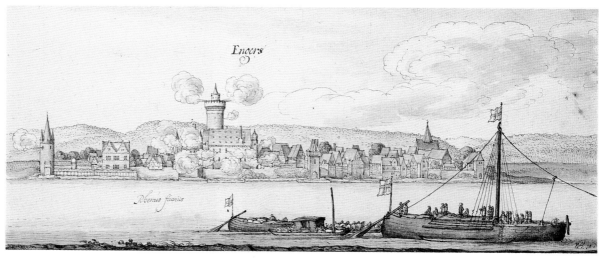

Plate 2. *The Rhine with the Town and Fortress of Engers.* Pen and watercolor. 1636. (no. 16)

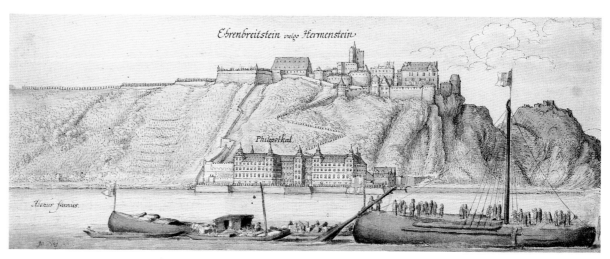

Plate 3. *Ehrenbreitstein on the Rhine.* Pen and watercolor. 1636. (no. 18)

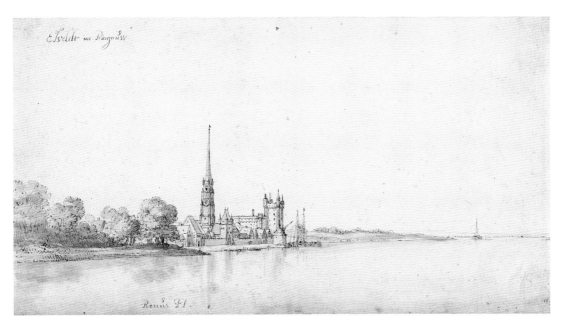

Plate 4. *View of Eltville on the Rhine.* Pen and brown ink with watercolor over traces of black chalk. (no. 20)

Plate 5. *A Public Execution at Linz.* Pen and watercolor. 1636. (no. 27)

Plate 6. *A Scene on the Danube, with the Monastery of Melk.* Pen and watercolor. 1636. (no. 28)

Plate 7. *London; Whitehall Palace.* Pen and ink, touched with watercolor. (no. 30)

Plate 8. *A Young Man with a Hideous Old Woman.* Etching. 1646. (no. 67)

Plate 9. *A Study of a Woman in Black, Wearing a Hood.* Oil on paper. (no. 90)

Plate 10. *Study of a Woman in Black, Wearing a Wide-Brimmed Hat.* Oil on paper. (no. 91)

Plate 11. *The Settlement at Whitby, West of Tangier.* Pen and ink with gray wash and watercolor. (no. 125)

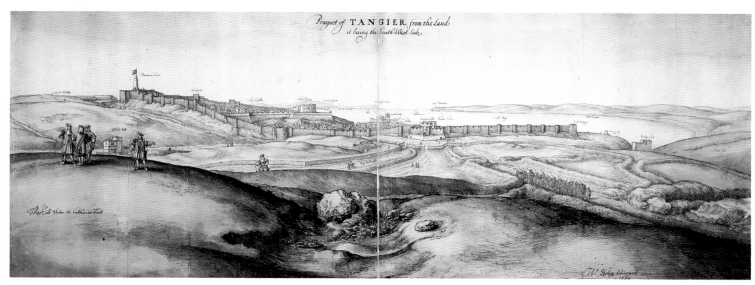

Plate 12. *Tangier from the South-West.* Pen and brown ink, with gray wash and watercolors. (no. 126)

Catalogue

In the catalogue entries, the abbreviation "P.," followed by a series of numbers, is from Gustav Parthey's *Wenzel Hollar: Beschreibendes Verzeichnis seiner Kupferstiche* (Berlin, 1852). Parthey arranged the material by subject, and his notation system was retained by Richard Pennington in his *Descriptive Catalogue of the Etched Works of Wenceslaus Hollar* (Cambridge, 1982). Pennington's authoritative introduction and catalogue are likely to remain definitive. The abbreviation "L." refers to Frits Lugt, *Les Marques de collections de dessins & d'estampes.* (Amsterdam, 1921, and The Hague, 1956). The following abbreviated references also are used in the catalogue:

Aubrey

Aubrey, John. *Aubrey's Brief Lives.* Ed. Oliver Lawson Dick. London, 1949.

Bartsch

Bartsch, Adam. *Le Peintre-graveur.* 21 vols. Vienna, 1803–1821.

Blum

Blum, Andre. *L'Oeuvre Gravé d'Abraham Bosse.* Paris, 1924.

Chaloner-Smith

Chaloner-Smith, J. *British Mezzotinto Portraits.* 4 vols. London, 1878–1883.

Croft-Murray and Hulton

Croft-Murray, Edward, and Paul Hulton. *Catalogue of British Drawings.* Vol. 1, *XVI & XVII Centuries.* London: British Museum, 1960.

Denkstein

Denkstein, Vladimir. *Hollar Drawings.* Prague, 1977; London, 1979 (in English).

Evelyn, *Diary*

Evelyn, John. *The Diary of John Evelyn.* 6 vols. Ed. E. S. Beer. Oxford, 1955.

Evelyn, *Fumifugium*

———. *Fumifugium: Or, The Inconvenience of the aer, And Smoke of London Dissipated.* London, 1661.

Evelyn, *Sculptura*

———. *Sculptura: or the History, and Art of Chalcography and Engraving in Copper.* London, 1662.

Fagan

Fagan, Louis. *A Descriptive Catalogue of the Engraved Works of William Faithorne.* London, 1888.

Hake

Hake, Henry M. "Some Contemporary Records Relating to Francis Place." *Walpole Society* 9 (1922): 39–69.

Hind

Hind, Arthur M. *Wenceslaus Hollar and His Views of London and Windsor in the Seventeenth Century.* London, 1922.

Hollstein

Hollstein, F. W. H. *Dutch and Flemish Etchings, Engravings and Woodcuts, ca. 1450–1700.* 60 vols. Amsterdam, 1949–1994.; and *German Engravings, Etchings and Woodcuts, ca. 1400–1700.* 35 vols. Amsterdam, 1953–1994.

Mauquoy-Hendrickx

Marie Mauquoy-Hendrickx, *L'Iconographie d'Antoine Van Dyck. Catalogue Raisonné* (Brussels, 1956).

Springell

Springell, Francis C. *Connoisseur & Diplomat. The Earl of Arundel's Embassy to Germany in 1636 as Recounted in William Crowne's Diary, the Earl's Letters and Other Contemporary Sources with a Catalogue of the Topographical Drawings Made on the Journey by Wenceslaus Hollar.* London, 1963.

Sprinzels

Sprinzels, Franz [Francis Springell]. *Hollars Handzeichnungen.* Vienna, 1938.

Vertue, *Description*

Vertue, George. *A Description of the Works of the Ingenious Delineator and Engraver Wenceslaus Hollar, Disposed into Classes of Different Sorts; With Some Account of His Life.* 2nd ed. London, 1759.

Vertue, "Note-Books"

———. "The Note-Books of George Vertue Relating to Artists and Collectors in England," *Walpole Society* 18 (1930).

White and Boon

White, Christopher, and Karel G. Boon. *Rembrandt van Rijn.* Vol. 18, F. W. H. Hollstein, *Dutch and Flemish Etchings, Engravings and Woodcuts.* Amsterdam, 1969.

1

AEGIDIUS SADELER (1570–1629)

The Vladislav Hall in the Hradčany Castle, Prague

Engraving (Hollstein 150)
1607
3573 × 320; 22½ × 12½

Metropolitan Museum of Art, New York, Harris Brisbane Dick Fund, 1953 (53.601.10[1])

This work was engraved and published in Prague in the year of Hollar's birth. Aegidius Sadeler worked in Prague from 1597 until his death in 1629. A fair is shown in progress in the flamboyantly vaulted great hall. At the lower left a print seller is displaying his stock to an interested client. The Vladislav Hall was—and still would be—a fine place to exhibit works of art because of the clear, natural light that floods in from the large windows at each side.

2

Fortune

Pen and ink (Sprinzels 83)
c. 1625
132 × 165; 5⅛ × 6½
Provenance: William Esdaile (L.2617)

Victoria and Albert Museum, London

If the inscribed date of 1625, added by a later hand, is correct, this is possibly Hollar's earliest surviving drawing. The subject of Fortune balancing on a globe above a stormy sea is an appropriate metaphor for travelers, and it may have a connection with Hollar's departure from Prague in 1627. The rather fussy, nervous technique of the penwork certainly suggests a very early date. At this time it is unlikely that Hollar had ever seen the sea, and his conception of vessels and waves owes much to prints after Brueghel and other Netherlandish masters. The figure of Fortune is borrowed from an engraving by Theodore de Bry in *Emblemata Nobilitati* . . . (Frankfurt, 1592–1593). This also served as the model for a miniature dated 1620 in a *Liber Amicorum* in the Narodni Galerie, Prague, which has been published by Denkstein as a very early work by Hollar.[1]

1. *Umeni* 29 (1981): 377–394.

A

B

C

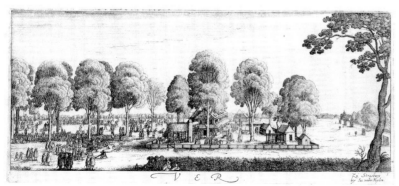

D

The Four Seasons: The Strasbourg Views

A SPRING; THE SHOOTING RANGE
B SUMMER; THE BATHING PLACE
C AUTUMN; THE WINE MARKET
D WINTER; THE PARADE GROUND

Etchings (P.622–P.625; first state of two)
Each plate: 106 × 245; 4⅛ × 9⅝

Dr. and Mrs. Howard A. Fox

These views etched in Strasbourg, probably in 1628 and 1629, represent different aspects of the city. They are among the most delicately worked of Hollar's early prints, and though they reflect the influence of the prints of Jan van de Velde, an individual touch is already visible, particularly in the soft molding of the contours of the trees in *Spring*. Hollar seems to have had fond memories of Strasbourg, and he returned to Strasbourg motifs at various points in his career.

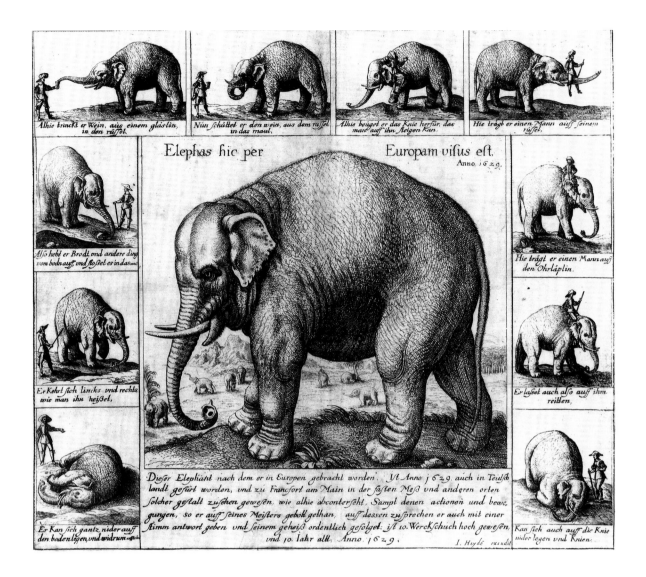

4

The Tame Elephant

Etching (P.2119)
1629
243 × 282; 9¾ × 11

Robert J. D. Harding

Etched in Strasbourg and published there by
Van der Heyden, this print borrows the
main figure of the elephant from a 1563
etching by Gerard von Groningen. The
enchanting side panels, however, which
demonstrate how to mount and ride an elephant, are Hollar's own designs.

See plate 1

The Wooden Gate at Düren

Pen and brown ink over black chalk, with brown, gray,
and pale green wash
Inscribed in an old hand, verso: "Die Holzpfort zu
Duren. W. Hollar"
102 × 186; 4 × 7¼
Provenance: Dr. H. Wellesly

Dr. and Mrs. Howard A. Fox

When he was based in Cologne, Hollar traveled to nearby Düren to make studies for a bird's-eye view of the town, which he etched in 1634 (P.841). He visited Düren again between 23 April and 22 May 1636 with the embassy of Arundel. This drawing must date from the earlier visit, when he made a number of drawings of the town and its environs, not all connected with the bird's-eye view.

Hollar seems to have retained an affection for Düren, as he did not etch this design until 1664 (P.733). Another etched view of Düren (P.732) is also of the same date. The subtle blending of line and wash shows Hollar's concern with atmosphere as well as topography.

6

The Thoroughfare

Etching (P.1239; second state of three)
105 × 198; 4 × 83

Dr. and Mrs. Howard A. Fox

It is likely that this view dates from the latter part of Hollar's German period. It is particularly notable for the delicacy with which he has rendered the elaborate fretwork of timber on the building in the center. The view has not been identified.

7

The Harbor at Amsterdam

Pen and ink with gray wash, tinted in watercolors
(Croft-Murray and Hulton 13)
1634
146 × 373; 5¾ × 14⅝
Provenance: Sir Thomas Lawrence (L. 2445); William
Esdaile (L.2617); purchased by the British Museum in
1862

British Museum, London; 1862-7-12-193

This view is taken from the south moat of
the city, looking north, with many vessels
visible in the harbor. In the middle distance
on the left is a partially dismasted ship in a
stockade. This carefully finished drawing
was made during Hollar's journey to Holland in 1634. He had a lifelong interest in
ships, and his visit to Amsterdam gave him
his first opportunity to study large oceangoing vessels.

8

Three Waves

Etching (P.1249; second state of three)
45 × 122; 1¾ × 4¾
Provenance: Hugh Melville Howard (L.1280b)

Dr. and Mrs. Howard A. Fox

This etching is from the series of eight small
seascapes (P.1248–P.1255), which are
undated but based on drawings Hollar made
in the Netherlands in 1634. The simplicity of
the design cannot disguise the artist's rap-
ture at what was most probably his first
sight of the open sea.

9

Rembrandt van Rijn (1606–1669)

Saskia with Pearls in Her Hair

Etching (Bartsch 347; White and Boon 347)
1634
87 × 68; 3½ × 2¾

Pierpont Morgan Library, New York; B347

This scarce portrait of Rembrandt's wife, Saskia, was given wider circulation by Hollar's copy in the *Reisbuchlein*. It is a moot point whether Hollar sought Rembrandt's permission to copy the print; seventeenth-century printmakers were often cavalier in their borrowing. Nevertheless, Hollar was at pains to acknowledge his source.

10

Bust of Saskia

Etching (P.1650; from the *Reisbuchlein* [P.1646–P.1669])
1636
67 × 54; 2⅝ × 2⅛

Frank W. Raysor II

The twenty-three small plates of the *Reisbuchlein* ("little travel book") were published by Abraham Hogenberg in Cologne in 1636. Most of the drawings must have been made in the Netherlands in 1634. This example is copied in reverse from Rembrandt's etching. It is a close copy, but Hollar has reduced the scale of the design to fit into the cramped format of the other prints in the series. He has also tidied up the freer etched lines of Rembrandt's original.

A

D

E

Strasbourg Views

A   THE TOLL HOUSE
Etching (P.701)
62 × 95; 2½ × 3¾

B   THE TOLL HOUSE
Etching (P.702)
61 × 95; 2¼ × 3¾

C   STRASBOURG
Etching (P.703)
61 × 95; 2¼ × 3¾

D   STRASBOURG
Etching (P.704)
62 × 95; 2½ × 3¾

E   HANAU
Etching (P.706)
62 × 95; 2½ × 3¾

Frank W. Raysor II

The Strasbourg views must be based on drawings Hollar made during his residence there in 1628 and 1629. He evidently retained an affection for the city where he had first commenced serious activity as an artist.

German Views

A Frankfurt
Etching (P.707)
62 × 95; 2½ × 3¾

B Rudesheim
Etching (P.708)
62 × 95; 2½ × 3¾

C Cologne
Etching (P.711)
62 × 95; 2½ × 3¾

Frank W. Raysor II

These and the preceding five plates are from
Amoenissimae aliquot locorum . . . effigies, a
collection of twenty-four etchings published
in 1635 in Cologne by Abraham Hogenberg.
The etchings are arranged according to the
sequence in which Hollar visited the
depicted sites, beginning in Prague and end-
ing in Holland.

A

B

C

13

Laughing Self-Portrait

Etching (P.1668)
1636
73 × 54; 2¾ × 2¼

Self-Portrait with Pointed Beard

Etching (P.1649)
1636
54 × 41; 2¼ × 1¾

Portrait of a Young Man

Etching (P.1669)
1636
50 × 43; 2 × 1¾

Christopher Mendez

All three of these male heads, published in the *Reisbuchlein*, were identified by George Vertue as self-portraits, but his only evidence seems to have been the resemblance of the first two to the Meyssens portrait etched by Hollar. Allowing for the difference in age, the resemblance does in fact seem close enough for the identification to be accepted, though *Portrait of a Young Man* clearly represents a different sitter.

It is possible that Hollar was influenced by the example of Rembrandt, whose etchings were fresh in his memory at this time. *Laughing Self-Portrait* brings to mind Aubrey's description of Hollar as a "very friendly good natured man as could be."

14

Woman Playing a Clavicord

Etching (P.594; second state of three)
1635
68 × 54; 2¾ × 2⅛
Provenance: John Evelyn

Dr. and Mrs. Howard A. Fox

The inscribed number "24" on this etching denotes its place at the end of the *Reisbuchlein.* The choice of such a genre subject must reflect Hollar's study of Dutch paintings of similar subjects when he was in Holland in 1634.

15

The Bowing Gentleman

Etching (P.1997; first state of two, before the address of
Hogenberg)
140 × 178; 5½ × 3
Provenance: Alfred Morrison (L.151)

Lady with a Houpette

Etching (P.1998; unrecorded proof before the name of
Hollar)
140 × 178; 5½ × 3
Provenance: Alfred Morrison (L.151)

Robert J. D. Harding

Published by Abraham Hogenberg in
Cologne between 1630 and 1636, these are
among Hollar's earliest and most accomplished costume plates. The lady wears a
houpette, a curious fluffy ball projecting
from her headpiece. This form of apparel
was found in Cologne and Antwerp.

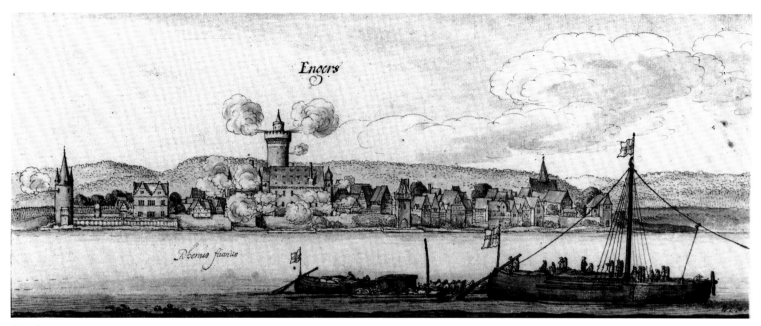

See plate 2

16

The Rhine with the Town and Fortress of Engers

Pen and watercolor (Sprinzels 118; Springell X)
1636 (dated "WH 10 M[ay]")
110 × 271; 4¼ × 10⅝

Duke of Devonshire and the Trustees of the
Chatsworth Settlement

The embassy sailed past Engers without
stopping as it headed down the Rhine
toward Coblenz. Cannons are firing from
the tower and in the town, as there were
hostilities between the French army and the
army of the emperor in this area.

17

The Rhine with Part of
Coblentz on the Left

Pen and watercolor 109 × 279; 4 ¼ × 11 (Sprinzels 189;
Springell XI)
1636 (dated "10 maij 1636")

A loading tower and a ship are seen by part of the town of Coblenz. Numerous batteries are firing from the fort of Hermenstein. Crowne recounts:

> Coblentz, a town adjoining the Rhine on the right, where the French had been recently driven out by the Emperor's forces into the Castle of Hermanstein, situated on a very high eminence opposite and overlooking the town. These forces were skirmishing when we arrived, consequently we cast anchor half a mile short of the town and sent a trumpeter to request a safe conduct for us. Passage was willingly granted, both sides interrupting the fight. The general in the town, making preparation to entertain His Excellency's entrance, but the forces in the castle immediately fired a cannon to the great danger of the town defenders, who now took cover until His Excellency actually appeared at the gate. He was hospitably entreated to dine there but, in view of the long journey planned for that day, he declined the invitation. As for those in the castle, they were besieged on every side, with cannons commanding the river bank in front of them, a great company of horsemen called Crabbats [Croats] behind them, and other cavalry and infantry on the extensive stretch of level ground beyond them. Other forces were stationed on islands in the Rhine whence they kept careful watch to prevent the possibility of relief, whilst if those inside the town chanced to look out of the windows, there was every likelihood that a bullet would whistle about their ears.

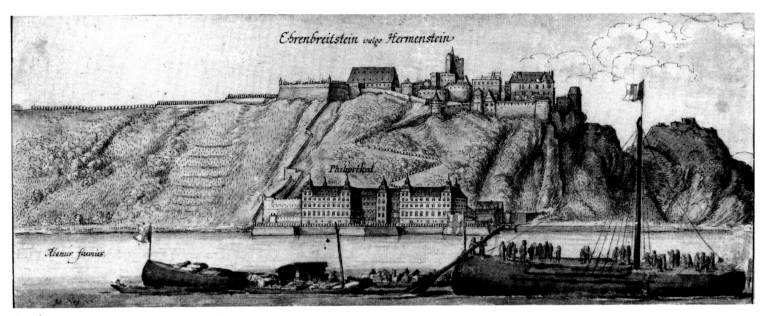

See plate 3

18

Ehrenbreitstein on the Rhine

Pen and watercolor (Sprinzels 190; Springell XII)
1636 (dated "10 Maij 1636")
109 × 279; 4¼ × 10¾

Duke of Devonshire and the Trustees of the
Chatsworth Settlement

This view on the Rhine shows the fort of
Ehrenbreitstein (or Hermenstein), with
Arundel's boat in the foreground. Hollar
has used a formalized division of tones to
differentiate the gray-tinted foreground
boats from the mountain and fort, which
are picked out in icy blue tones. This drawing is closely related to an etching (P.709)
showing a view across the Rhine from
Coblenz but omitting Arundel's barges.
Other sketches of this spectacular fort, its
ramparts lined with soldiers, are in a Hollar
sketchbook in the John Rylands Library,
Manchester.

19

The Rhine with the Mauseturn in the Middle Distance

Pen and watercolor (Sprinzels 202; Springell XXV)
1636 (dated "2/12 maij 1636")
106 × 235; 4⅛ × 9¼

Duke of Devonshire and the Trustees of the
Chatsworth Settlement

Arundel's boat, pulled by a team of horses,
is in the foreground. Crowne noted, "We
entered Meientzisches Land, passing a little
tower in the water called the Mouse Tower,
built by a certain Bishop Otto, who had
lived an unhappy life plagued by mice and
who thought that in that tower he would be
secure from them. The story goes that even
here they pursued him and finally eat him."

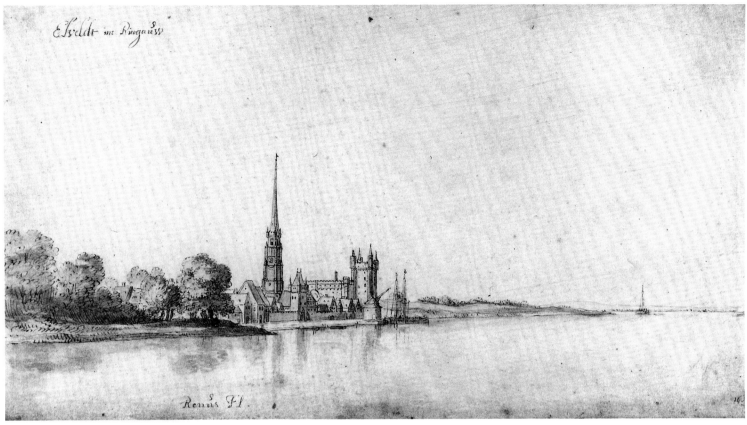

Eltfeldt im: Ringauss

Renus Fl.

See plate 4

20

View of Eltville on the Rhine

Pen and brown ink with watercolor over traces of black chalk
167 × 307; 6⁹⁄₁₆ × 12⅛

Yale Center for British Art, Paul Mellon Fund; B1986.26

The embassy of the Earl of Arundel passed through Eltville on 2 May 1636. Hollar presumably made a sketch on the spot and used it as a basis for this drawing and for another similar view of Eltville in the Kupferstichkabinett, Berlin. The Berlin drawing is longer in format and more worked up with the pen, but it lacks the limpid simplicity of the Yale drawing, with its delicately painted reflections in the water.

21

The Rhine with Cologne in the Background

Pen and watercolor (Springell I)
110 × 567; 4⅜ × 22¼

Confluence of the Rhine and the Main

Pen and watercolor (Springell XXXV)
101 × 562; 4 × 22

Nuremberg

Pen and watercolor (Springell XLVI)
111 × 524; 4⅜ × 20⅝

Duke of Devonshire and the Trustees of the Chatsworth Settlement

These three panoramamic views are among the most advanced of Hollar's early drawings, the prospect of Mainz given additional piquancy by the artist's depiction of himself seated drawing in the center of the design. The female figures at the side of the view of Nuremberg anticipate the many etchings of costume that Hollar was to make in England. The calligraphy of the lettering in the Nuremberg drawing is of particular exuberance and is used to set off the hillocks of curved earth in the foreground. To some extent these drawings seem to be independent in function from other drawings made on the embassy.

Moenus fluvius

22

Aschaffenberg on the Main

Pen and watercolor (Sprinzels 215; Springell XL)
1636 (dated "18/28 Maij 1636")
132 × 274; 5¼ × 10¾

Duke of Devonshire and the Trustees of the
Chatsworth Settlement

This drawing, entirely devoid of landscape
elements, is the most particularized architectural drawing that Hollar made on the
embassy.

23

Deggendorf on the Danube

Graphite and black ink
1636
60 × 229; 2⅜ × 9
Provenance: Sir Bruce Ingram (L. Supplement 1405a)

Pierpont Morgan Library, New York

This is a sketch for a finished watercolor drawing now in the National Gallery at Prague (Sprinzels 233; Denkstein 40). It shows the boats of Arundel's embassy on the Danube near Deggendorf. It seems possible that the pen lines were added later to supplement a graphite sketch made from life, by necessity at lightning speed.

24

Straubing on the Danube

Pen and watercolor (Sprinzels 231; Springell LII)
1636
111 × 275; 4⅜ × 10¾

Duke of Devonshire and the Trustees of the Chatsworth Settlement

The embassy stayed for a single night at Straubing while en route to Linz. The members of Arundel's retinue stand with heads bared as the earl prepares to board the vessel.

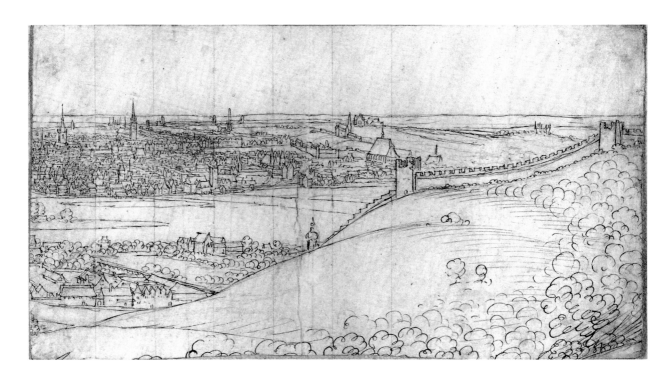

25

View of Prague from the Laurentiusberg

Pen and gray ink over black chalk (Sprinzells 274)
123 × 235; 4¾ × 9½
Provenance: Francis Springell (Sotheby's, London, 30 June 1986, lot 13)

Frank W. Raysor II

This is almost certainly a drawing made on the spot when Hollar visited Prague with Arundel's Embassy between 6 and 13 July 1636. Hollar utilized it for his finished drawing, the *Great Prospect of Prague* (National Gallery, Prague). The view is taken looking across the river to the so-called "Old Town" from a vantage point near the Hradcany Castle.

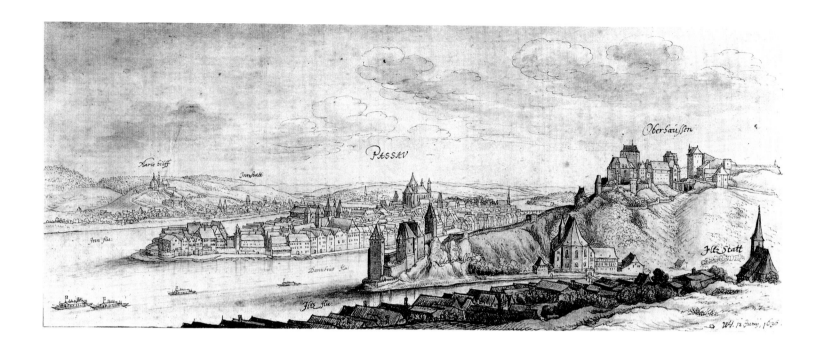

26

The Great Prospect of Passau

Pen and gray ink, with grayish-green and brownish-pink wash (Sprinzels 248)
1636 (signed and dated "12 Junij 1636")
109 × 274; 4¼ × 10¾
Provenance: Jonathan Richardson, Sr. (L.2983), his sale, London, Covent Garden, 22 January 1745, part of lot 45, £1/10s; Francis Springell, Sotheby's, London, 30 June 1986, lot 8

Pierpont Morgan Library, New York; purchased as the gift of Mrs. Charles Wrightsman; 1986.36

Passau

Etching (P.744)
61 × 140; 2⅜ × 5½

Passau

Etching (P.745)
61 × 140; 2⅜ × 5½

Dr. and Mrs. Howard A. Fox

The highly finished drawing was evidently worked up later from sketches made on the spot, since Arundel's embassy had left Passau on 4 June, and on Sunday, 12 June, it was resting at Linz. Another elaborate drawing of Passau, seen from the opposite direction, is in the Fitzwilliam Museum, Cambridge. This spectacular location was described by Crowne: "Passau, which is just beyond Bavaria, has a very pleasing position, with three rivers running by the city; the Danube, grey in colour, flows past one side; the white waters of the swift-running Inn, which rises in Italy, sweep past another side; while on the third side are the black waters of the Ilz, flowing out of Bohemia, and like the Inn, joins the Danube just beyond the town."

Hollar was not the first artist to respond to this epic vista. N. G. Stogdon has established that a celebrated etching of 1546 by Augustin Hirschvogel (Hollstein 45) is a view in reverse of the northern part of Passau.[1] Hirschvogel's view, in keeping with the traditions of the Danube school of etchers, is spiky and agitated, whereas Hollar emphasizes the panoramic sweep.

It is to be regretted that Hollar never translated the whole sheet into an etching, confining himself to the small etching (P.744) of the right-hand part of the view from a slightly different angle. This and P.745 belong to a group of twelve etchings of German views that are undated but presumably were executed in England.

1. N. G. Stogdon, *Catalogue IX, German Landscapes of the 16th Century*, no. 20 (London, 1993).

See plate 5

27

A Public Execution at Linz

Pen and watercolor (Sprinzels 259; Springell LXXXI)
129 × 274; 5⅛ × 10¾
Dated: 20 Junij 1636
Provenance: Wellesley Collection; the Reverend J. J.
Heywood

Duke of Devonshire and the Trustees of the
Chatsworth Settlement

Public executions were frequent events during the Thirty Years War and commonly the subjects of prints. Hollar was possibly influenced by Claes Jansz Visscher's well-known *Execution of Arminians in the Hague* (Hollstein 46), published in 1623, and the subject of at least two etched copies. This is one of the few drawings Hollar made on the Arundel embassy that explicitly describe the barbaric horrors on every side.

Crowne described the event in his *Diary* on 10 June 1636:

> On this same day, seven rebels, the leaders of an armed insurrection of 400 ignorant peasants against the Emperor were beheaded. The ringleader of the revolt, a fellow who had persuaded himself that no bullet had power to harm him, was led onto the scaffold with his face covered and with two men holding him firmly against the block. Here the executioners seized him firmly by the chest with a massive pair of red-hot pincers and, nailing his right hand to the block, chopped it off. Then, quickly drawing the sword he wore at his side, he cut off the wretched fellow's head which an assistant raised, shouting into the ears of the dead man: "JESUS, JESUS." At this juncture the Jesuit, who had accompanied the criminal and who had been admonishing him for his sins, asked those present to join in prayer for the soul of the dead man. Following this came the man's accomplices, including a young boy, all of whom bore crucifixes in their hands and made their individual confessions at the foot of the scaffold to priests, kissing their hands and feet at the end of every prayer. After these wretches had been beheaded and quartered, two of their confederates were taken on foot about a mile to a place where the body of a priest of theirs, arrested the previous year in the church of ERING, hung on a pole.

Hollar's drawing agrees in many particulars with this description. The unfortunates at the foot of the scaffolding appear to have made their confessions while shrouded in the gowns of their confessors, a spectacle suggesting some horrible subject by Goya.

See plate 6

28

A Scene on the Danube, with the Monastery of Melk

Pen and watercolor (Sprinzels 267; Springell XC)
119 × 273; 4¾ × 10¾

Duke of Devonshire and the Trustees of the
Chatsworth Settlement

In the background can be seen a boat pulled
by a long procession of horses, a sight frequently remarked by the English travelers.
The interaction of the regular contours of
the boat in the foreground with
the curved bank of earth is especially
mellifluous.

29

CLAUDE DE JONGH (ca. 1600–1663)

The Thames at Westminster Stairs

Oil on panel
1637
464 × 800; 18¼ × 31½

Yale Center for British Art, Paul Mellon
Collection; B1973.1.31

The Dutch artist Claude de Jongh is best
remembered for a small group of paintings
of London, which he painted in Holland
from drawings made in England in 1627 and
without overmuch concern for topographical accuracy. Westminster Abbey is seen on
the right, hemmed in by buildings. The
painting is notable for its curiously dirgelike
atmosphere; the buildings seeming petrified
with age. The river itself, with a few sluggish
craft, entirely lacks the animation that Hollar habitually gave to such scenes; however,
de Jongh remains an important pioneer of
London views.

See plate 7

30

London; Whitehall Palace

Pen and ink, touched with watercolor (Croft-Murray
and Hulton 7)
98 × 293; 3⅞ × 11⅝

British Museum, London; 1859–8-6–389

This view, taken from south of the river,
shows part of Lambeth marshes at the left.
The Banqueting House dominates the center of the skyline, with the buildings of
Whitehall Palace around it. The water is
crowded with boats carrying passengers, a
reminder that the Thames was the main
thoroughfare of London, and passenger-
carrying wherries were almost as numerous
as black cabs today. The Banqueting House,
London's newest and grandest building at
the time of Hollar's arrival in 1636, appears
in many of his etchings. This drawing appears to be an independent sheet, but a
more worked-up study of the central area of
Whitehall may have served as the basis of
the etching *Palatio Regis prope. Londinum
vulgo Whitehall* (P.1039).

31

View of Westminster and the Thames from Lambeth House

Pen and brown ink over graphite (Croft-Murray and Hulton 5)
151 × 401; 6 × 15¼

British Museum, London; 1882–8-12–224

This view looks north down the river, from near Lambeth Stairs, which are visible on the right. On the far bank can be seen Westminster Abbey, Westminster Hall, and Whitehall. Lambeth Palace is on the right. In the foreground is a cluster of wherries, one of which is about to put off, while another has just disgorged its passengers. Although the figures are tiny, they are deftly characterized, notably the figure of a woman who gathers her skirts and walks briskly up the wooden gangplank. Hollar particularly enjoyed drawing these busy embarkation points, and this drawing is comparable in type to his etching of *Lambeth from Whitehall* (P.912). This drawing must have been made during his first English period, between 1637 and 1644.

32

Greenwich

Etching on two plates (P.977; first state of four)
1637
154 × 844; 6 × 33¼

British Museum, London; 1855–6-9–23

In this first state, as issued by Hollar, the plate bears a dedication to Queen Henrietta Maria that was removed when her popularity in the country waned. One of Hollar's largest and grandest prints, it announced the establishment in England of a landscape artist of a sophistication with which the country had little experience. In the middle distance can be seen the Queen's House, originally commissioned from Inigo Jones by Anne of Denmark and begun in 1616 but completed only in 1635. Atop the hill on the left is a royal lodge, later rebuilt and established as the Royal Observatory. Beyond the Queen's House is the old Tudor palace of Greenwich. The rolling lines of the landscapes are characteristic of Hollar and tailored to his needs without undue veracity to the actual appearance of the land. In the first state the sky is clear; later, perhaps with prescience of the monarchy's decline, he introduced dark clouds.

Before leaving England in 1644 Hollar sold the plates to the print seller Peter Stent. Impressions bearing Stent's name can be of very high quality, suggesting that not many impressions had been taken earlier.

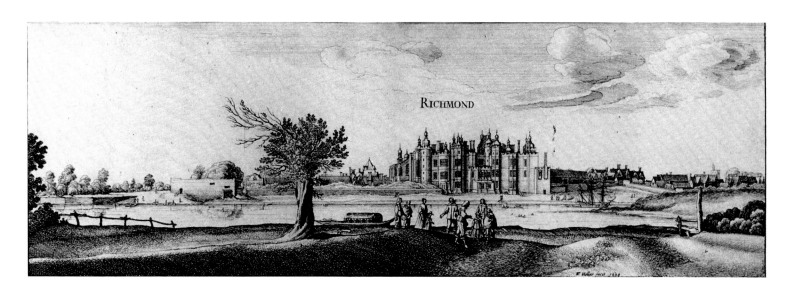

33

Richmond Palace

Etching (P.1058)
1638
115 × 338; 4½ × 13¼

Metropolitan Museum of Art, New York, Rogers Fund, 1920; 20.81.2(4)

This is sometimes described as a copy of a practically identical print by Hollar, but I share Pennington's belief that the quality is so high that it is virtually impossible for it to be by any other hand than Hollar's. Perhaps an accident occurred with the first plate, necessitating the execution of another version. The principal change is the introduction of a large "G" on the banner of the ship in the background at right.

Richmond Palace was founded in 1499 by Henry VII and became one of the most favored residences of the Tudor monarchs. Queen Elizabeth died there in 1603. Prince Henry and his younger brother Charles, later to become Charles I, used it to house much of their vast art collections. It was neglected during the Commonwealth and largely demolished in the reign of Queen Anne.

In the foreground, a man—strongly resembling Hollar's early print of the *Bowing Gentleman* (no. 15)—makes obeisance to two small boys. They have seemingly emerged with other stately figures from the barge moored on the bank. It is by no means impossible that they represent the royal family and that the bowing man is saluting Prince Charles and his younger brother James, later to become Charles II and James II.

Charles by the grace of God, Kinge of England, Scotland, France and Ireland, defendor of the faith, etc:

Henrietta Maria by the Grace of God, Queene of England, Scotland, France, and Ireland, etc:

W. Hollar. fecit Londini, 1641.

34

King Charles I and Queen Henrietta Maria

Etching (P.1416; first state)
1641
176 × 244; 6⅞ × 9⅝

Metropolitan Museum of Art, New York, Gift of Mason Chikin, 1952; 52.614

This is an impression of the first state, before the plate was cut into two separate portraits, with the lettering of "Henrica" changed by pen to "Henrietta." This plate was published without any form of royal privilege, suggesting that it was an independent venture without the sanction of the king. The composition derives loosely and without acknowledgment from a Van Dyck portrait of the king and queen that was once in the Royal Collection and is now at Státni Zámek, Kroměřítz, Slovakia. The portrait of the king from the cut-down plate was used in *The True Effigies of . . . King Charles* (London, 1641). The removal of the queen from the plate may have been the result of her increasing unpopularity in the country, because of her avowed Catholicism. The dedicatory inscription to her on Hollar's plate of Greenwich was also removed, probably for the same reason.

35

Seleucus and His Son

Etching (P.527)
1637
285 × 377; 11¼ × 14⅞

Robert J. D. Harding

The subject illustrated here is the legend of Seleucus Nicator (358–280 B.C.), the ruler of an eastern province of the empire of Alexander the Great. His son, an adulterer, was condemned to lose both of his eyes, but Seleucus saved one of his son's eyes by volunteering to have one of his own plucked out.

The print derives from a drawing then in the Arundel collection that was dedicated to Arundel (fig. 9). The lines, by Henry Peacham, urge us to note the virtuous example of Seleucus. The original from which Hollar's image ultimately derives is a fresco, possibly by Ronaldo Mantovano, after a design by Guilio Romano for the Casino della Grotta, Palazzo del Te, at Mantua. The drawing used by Hollar is probably one that is now in the British Museum, where it is classed by Pouncey and Gere among copies of Romano and others "of little or no interest which it has not been thought necessary to catalogue."

It is indeed a drawing of manifestly poor quality; moreover, it is in reverse to Romano's original, suggesting that it may have been copied from an unknown engraving or possibly freely adapted from Antonio Fantuzzi's etching, which is in reverse to the original.[1] Hollar's etching is in reverse to the British Museum drawing (fig. 7), thus unwittingly bringing the design back to its original sense, with Seleucus indicating his left eye as the one to be sacrificed.

Some interesting problems are posed by Hollar's selection of a mediocre drawing of an obscure and gruesome subject for such an important dedicatory print. Was the difference in scholarship so great that he (and Arundel) believed this to be one of the great drawings in the collection? Did the print have some more personal meaning in which it was the subject of the drawing that counted, not its quality? It is possible that the subject offers an appropriate allusion to Arundel's sense of paternal duty.

It is well known that Hollar had some defect in his left eye. Arundel seems to have remembered this fact (if not the artist's name) when, close to his death in Padua, he asked the visiting John Evelyn "to use all meanes to procure the little booke for me designed by the one eyed sculptor as I wrote." There remains the possibility that Hollar was making a reference, comprehensible only to those who knew him, to his own ocular deficiency, which Seleucus is about to share.

1. Henri Zerner, *Ecole de Fontainebleau: Gravures* (Paris, 1969), 11.

36

A Pagan Sacrifice

Etching (P.465)
1638
260 × 185; 10¼ × 7¼

Frank W. Raysor II

The original drawing was in the Arundel
collection, where it was attributed to Mantegna; it is now in the Hermitage, St. Peters-
burg.[1] The attribution to Mantegna has long
been abandoned, and the drawing has been
variously attributed to Francesco Francia or
to an artist of the fifteenth-century Venet-
ian-Lombard school, perhaps with some
knowledge of Mantegnaesque prototypes. It
is related in subject to a drawing by Francia
in the Pierpont Morgan Library. Irrespective
of its subject and attribution, the design
must have proved congenial to Hollar; the
jutting poles held by two of the figures give
the composition the structural scaffolding
used by the artist in a number of his maritime subjects. The print is in the reverse
direction to the drawing, and there is a
counterproof in the Fitzwilliam Museum.

1. Marzia Faietti and Konrad Oberhuber, *Bologna E
L'Umanesimo 1490–1510* (Bologna, 1988), 256.

Andrea Mantegnio inu: W. Hollar, fecit. 1638. Secundum Originale quod conseruatur in Ædibus Arundelianis Londini.

37

Richard II Presenting the Banner of Saint George to the Virgin Mary and the Infant Jesus (The Wilton Diptych)

Etching, on two plates (P.229a, P.229b)
1639
Each plate 250 × 140; 8¾ × 5 ½

Private collection

This important pair of etchings was dedicated to Charles I by Hollar and is inscribed with a royal privilege. The Latin inscription below, with details of the Plantagenet dynasty, was written by Henry Peacham, who furnished a number of inscriptions for important etchings by Hollar.

The original painting (fig. 10), by an unidentified artist of the late fourteenth century, entered the collection of Charles I in 1639, and Hollar etched it in the same year. Atypically, he has preserved the correct direction of the composition. The first queen of Richard II was Anne of Bohemia, and the sister of Charles I, Elizabeth, was the wife of the ill-starred Frederick V of Bohemia. It seems certain that Hollar, who prominently notes his Bohemian nationality at the end of the dedication, was using this connection to attract the king's attention.

Richard II kneels at the left, flanked by John the Baptist, Edward the Confessor, and King Edmund. He has just presented to the infant Jesus the banner of St. George, a symbolic gift of the kingdom of England. Recent research has revealed a tiny map of England, set in a silver sea, painted on the orb at the top of the banner.[1] It is almost inconceivable that Hollar, with his love of maps, would not have shown this in some way, and it seems likely that this detail had been lost sight of by the time the picture entered the collection of the king.

The picture is known as *The Wilton Diptych* because it was in the collections of the Earls of Pembroke at Wilton House before entering the National Gallery in London.

1. Dillian Gordon, "A New Discovery in *The Wilton Diptych*," *Burlington Magazine* (October 1993): 662–667.

Tabulam hanc olim ab ANDREA MANTENIO cum penna delineatam, et nunc
Londini in Ædibus Arundelianis conseruatam. Wenceslaus Hollar, Bohem, aqua forti incidit.

The Large Chalice

Etching (P.2543)
1640
271 × 174; 10⅝ × 6⅞

Yale Center for British Art, Paul Mellon
Collection; B1977.14.11750

When in Arundel's collection, the large
drawing reproduced by this etching was
attributed to Mantegna (fig. 7). The size of
the print (almost to scale with the drawing)
and the care with which the drawing was
copied suggest the regard in which it was
held. The etching technique is of great virtuosity, following every loop of the pen in the
original.

The drawing, which is on vellum, is now
in the British Museum and is attributed to
an anonymous northern Italian artist.

The Holy Family

Etchings (P.134)
1642
215 × 165; 8½ × 6½
Provenance: Formerly in the Royal Collection.
Inscribed *The Queen's Dupl*[icate] in pencil in the hand of Frederick Nicolay, Royal Music Librarian to Queen Charlotte during the 1770s.

Robert J. D. Harding

Copied from a drawing attributed to Perino del Vaga then in the Arundel collection. The rendering of the flowing lines of the drapery in Perino del Vaga's drawing is vivacious but, as usual, controlled. The inscriptions are particularly full and informative, suggesting that the drawing was considered of particular importance. The print is dedicated to Jerome Lanier and was published by Hendrick van der Borcht; it is one of the very few Hollar prints published by him in England. The print is also one of the few of Hollar's first English period to bear a royal privilege.

The provenance is of great interest, showing that the number of Hollars in the Royal Collection was so large at this date that duplicates could be disposed of.

Baſia; blanda VENVS, mea ſunt, et mollia cuncta,
Quam donabat amans, chirog, theca, manu,

Loves dalliance, kiſes and what ere is ſoft,
   Are mine, so are theſe gloves my lover bought

40

Woman Wearing a Tall, Dark Hat

Etchings (P.1734; first, second, and third states)
1638
Each plate: approximately 192 × 95; 7½ × 3¾

British Museum, London

The history of this plate and its presumed companions is very curious. The unique impression of the first state in the British Museum is signed and dated by Hollar, and it is unquestionably an authentic work of very high quality. In the second state, also rare, the signature is erased and an amorous inscription added: *Basia, blanda Venus, mea sunt. et mollia cuncta/Quam donabat amans.* (Love's dalliance, kisses and what ere is soft,/Are mine, so are these gloves my lover bought.) In the third state (unique impression) these lines are removed, and the plate acquires the address of Peter Stent, whose business commenced in about 1644.

It is evident that at some stage the plate passed out of Hollar's control, and the erasure of the signature suggests that he disowned it. In 1638 he was straining to establish himself and to gain the approbation not only of Arundel but also of the king. The design is, by Caroline standards, mildly erotic in flavor and not best calculated to advance his status as a serious artist. It is possible, therefore, that the two later states of the print were issued against the artist's will or without his knowledge. The problem is compounded by two prints evidently intended as its companions: *Woman with a Pearl Necklace* (P. 1732) and *Woman with Her Hands in a Muff* (P.1733). Both were published by Stent in the same octagonal format, and the former is inscribed in the second state "W. Hollar fecit." However, the signature is not his, the quality is poor, and there is every possibility that both prints are contemporary forgeries of his work. A fourth print published by Stent in the same format shows *Lady at the Virginals* (P.1735). This is unsigned but certainly by Hollar, and it was used on the title page of William Byrd's *Parthenia* in 1651.

This tangled web suggests the complexities of the contemporary print trade and the trickery of which some publishers were capable.

41

Ornatus Muliebris Anglicanus—or—The Severall Habits of English Women from the Nobilitie to the Country Woman, as They Are in These Times

Etchings (P.1778–P.1803; title page and twenty-six plates, the title page the first state of seven, the plates in the state with the numbers)
1638–1640
Each plate: approximately 135 × 74; 5½ × 2⅞

Robert J. D. Harding

Unlike the *Aula Veneris,* this series is devoted solely to the costume of English women. The first sixteen plates depict ladies of the highest fashion wearing the grandest clothes that Caroline costumiers could provide. Plates seventeen to twenty-five show women smartly dressed—scarcely decked out with the splendor required by the court, but in a style more than adequate for the more sober requirements of the city. The final figure, turning her back on her fair predecessors in the set, is a peasant woman with a basket of vegetables, whom Hollar has deliberately etched in a more severe style. The plates have been arranged with great care so that the poses rotate and complement each other.

Many of the poses of the more fashionable figures are generally indebted to Van Dyck, and some specifically so, though the reversal of the figures in the prints disguises their sources (as it was perhaps intended to do). Thus plate 7 is taken from *Mary Villiers, Duchess of Lenox and Richmond* (fig. 11; North Carolina Museum of Art), plate 8 from *Martha, Countess of Monmouth* (England, private collection), and plate 11 from *A Lady of the Spencer Family* (Tate Gallery). The faces are generalized, but the details of drapery are very close to the originals, and it is evident that Hollar had access to Van Dyck's studio over a period of years, and, presumably, permission to make sketches.

Hollar's copper plates passed through the hands of many print publishers, including Peter Stent and Henry Overton, and impressions are often worn and inferior. Early uniform sets are very scarce, and the present example is of marvelous quality and uniformity.

42

Aula Veneris

A TITLE PAGE (P.1805; second state of four)
B NOBILIS MULIER BOHEMICA (P.1806; first
   state of two)
C MULIER COLONIENSIS (P.1842; first state of
   two)
D MULIER NOBILIS HISPANICA (P.1878; only
   state)
E NOBILIS MULIER ANGLICA (P.1884; second
   state of three)
F MULIER GENEROSA ANGLICA (P.1888;
   fourth state of four)
G CIVIS LONDINENSIS UXOR (P.1894; fifth
   state of five)
H MULIER SCOTICA (P.1899; first state of two)

Etchings (P.1804–P.1907)
Each plate: approximately 93 × 58; ¾ × 2¼

Frank W. Raysor II

Mulier Coloniensis.

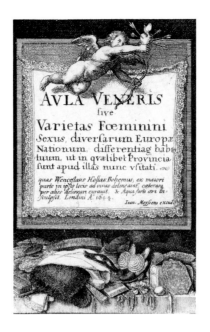

Ein Schpanische Dam.

Mulier Nobilis Hispanica.

English: Gentle: woman

Mulier Generosa Anglica.

These miniature costume plates were probably planned even before Hollar came to
England in 1636. They were worked on and
issued in various sets through his first
period in England and his resettlement in
Antwerp in 1644. They retained their popularity, and the plates were still being used in
the nineteenth century. The present title
page bears the name of the Antwerp publisher Meyssens, but in the first state it bears
the name and London address of Hollar in
1644.

   Aula Veneris was not a single coherent
published set but a project that was continually augmented, and a number of plates
bear English titles in their first state and
German ones later as Hollar adapted to a
Continental audience. His purpose was to
provide a convenient guide to the whole
range of contemporary female costume,
from the courts of Europe to the wilderness
of Virginia, and he had to rely not only on
his own drawings and recollections but also
on the prints and drawings of others.

43

The Four Seasons: The Three-Quarter-Length Figures

Etchings (P.610; Pennington's third state of four, with the address "F.L.D. Il Ciartres excudit, Cum Priu: regis Christianissimi"; P.611–P.613, first state of two)
1641
Each plate: approximately 250 × 179; 9¾ × 7

Private collection

The publishing history of this series is curious. Pennington describes as a first state of *Spring* an impression at Windsor, perhaps unique, with the address of Robert Peake in "his shop neere Holborne Conduit." He notes a second state, also apparently unique, in the Fisher collection at Montreal with Peake's address erased. His third state is that of this example, with the name of Ciartes. This was the assumed name of François Langlois of Chartres, a Parisian etcher and print publisher who was painted in the guise of a bagpiper by both Van Dyck and Claude Vignon. Pennington believed that Ciartres was precluded as the publisher of the first state by the impossibility of Hollar's plates being in Paris. In 1641, however, Ciartres was in London in the winter, and it is perfectly possible that he had a number of impressions printed off with his name for distribution in Paris. Langlois had several connections with England. He was sometimes employed as an agent by Arundel, and at one stage he tried to persuade the great French engraver Claude Mellan to come to England. He published in Paris prints by Callot and was also the publisher of Abraham Bosse's series of fashion plates *Le Jardin de la Noblesse*, a 1629 work that seems to have influenced Hollar and which is similar, in its engrossment with the fashionable world, to these prints by Hollar.

A SPRING

The woman holds tulips in her left hand, and gestures to a vase of flowers with her right. At the right corner is a wooden box with a fur muff partially inserted. This signifies the end of winter, when expensive furs were locked away to protect them from moths. Beyond the window is a country house with an ornamental garden. It is most unlikely that the vase of flowers was drawn from life. It resembles instead ornamental Netherlandish flower prints, or even the paintings of Bosschaert, examples of which were in the Arundel collection.

B SUMMER

The figure is very fashionably dressed, with a veil, a fan, and elaborate slashed sleeves. Two cooling melons are on the table. The long gloves are intended to protect the complexion of her hands. Beyond is the Thames with a distant view of Lambeth and Westminster, as seen from the vicinity of Arundel House.

C AUTUMN

The costume of the figure is accentuated by the plain background, which contrasts with the windows of the previous prints. She is distractedly handling a dish of fruit.

D WINTER

The woman clutches her collar with her gloved right hand, and her left hand is encased in a muff. Other furs and a mask are on the windowsill.

44

The Four Seasons: The Full-Length Figures

Etchings (P.606, second state of two; P.607–P.609, first state)
1643–1644
Each plate: 265 × 185; 10¼ × 7¼

Private collection

Etched in London between 1643 (*Spring* and *Winter*) and 1644 (*Summer* and *Autumn*), this was the last important series that Hollar completed before he went to Antwerp in 1644. The monumental scale of the fashionably clad figures, who stand on platforms raised above the landscapes and townscapes beyond, owes something to the example of Jacques Callot, especially his set of *Three Italian Comedians*[1] dated to 1618–1620. They are among the grandest of Hollar's compositions, particularly in the assurance with which the contours of the figures are expressed. A small technical flaw in *Winter*—partial failure in printing of the most densely worked dark areas—is to be noted in nearly all impressions. This defect was remedied in the etched series *Muffs* (no. 92).

A SPRING

A fashionably dressed woman clutches her skirts with her left hand and a bunch of tulips in her right. The extraordinary craze for speculating in tulips was rampant at this time. The identity of the elegant building in the background, with enclosed ornamental gardens, has remained a matter of dispute. Graham Parry notes that it has been tentatively identified as Tart Hall, the residence of the Countess of Arundel, built for her and completed by Nicholas Stone in 1638 near the site of the present Buckingham Palace. Certainly in 1643 this building would have had special significance for Hollar, since his first child, James, was born in Tart Hall that year. Elias Ashmole records this in an astrological note in his manuscripts in the Bodleian Library (Ms.3) "James Hollar filius Wenceslai [?] Holler nat. 5 8 April hor [?] 2 mane anno 1643 apud Tart Hall." This, and not Arundel House, was presumably the family residence at the time.

B SUMMER

A woman is seen in profile, stirring the air with a fan in her left hand. Her complexion is protected by a beautifully etched veil. The view beyond shows St. James's Park, with the new Inigo Jones building, the Banqueting House, and Old St. Paul's Cathedral. The luscious landscape and serene clear sky

may not be entirely fanciful. The curse of the London atmosphere was sea-coal, brought by sea from Newcastle. In 1644, however, Newcastle was besieged and could not export coal. John Evelyn notes in *Fumifugium* that, as a consequence, London had a bounteous summer, with rich summer foliage and an unusual abundance of fruit.

C Autumn

She holds a small fan, attached by a cord to the top of her apron. Her clothing, though fine, is less rich than that of the other figures. Beyond is an elegant landscape, with a semi-ruined classical building; a vine-covered wall is at the left. This is

Albury in Surrey, the much-loved country retreat of the Earl of Arundel.

D Winter

Richly clad in furs, she stands before a London view of Cornhill, with the tower of the Royal Exchange at right. The little structure

As Autumnes fruit doth mourne and wast   So of herselfe (she feares) she shall,
And if not pluckt it dropps at last Autumne If not timely gather'd, fall.

The cold, not cruelty makes her weare Winter For a smoother skinn at night,
In Winter, furrs and Wild beastshaire   Embraceth her with more delight.

at the extreme right was known as the Tun.
Built in 1283, it served as a lockup for drunks
and other miscreants. The plumes of smoke
are elegant and ornamental, and give little
idea of the extreme pollution of London's
atmosphere.

1. J. Lieure, *Jacques Callot. Catalogue de l'Oeuvre Gravé*
(Paris, 1924), 288–290.

45

Abraham Bosse (1602–1676)

La Galerie du Palais

Etching (Blum 1065)
c. 1640
248 × 315; 9¾ × 12⅜

Metropolitan Museum of Art, New York, Rogers
Fund, 1922; 22.67.16

Bosse and Hollar must have been familiar
with each other's work, sharing as they did a
predilection for fashionable costume and
accoutrements. In the center a man and
three well-clad women are examining a display of fans. The neighboring stalls contain
books, at the left, and lace, at the right. At
the extreme right an assistant is tying a par-
cel, perhaps a purchase of lace made by the
ladies in the center.

Bosse used a regulated method of etching
mixed with engraving, which is more
mechanical than the etched technique of
Hollar.

46

The Winter Habit of an English Gentlewoman

Etching (P.1999)
1644
213 × 107; 8⅜ × 4¼

Metropolitan Museum of Art, New York, Gift of
Theodore de Wit, 1923; 23.65.35

A richly clad and befurred women eyes us
impassively from behind her mask. However, she would have been considered ill
bred had she not removed the mask when
she saw friends or acquaintances on the
street. Pennington has pointed out that the
signature and inscription are not in Hollar's
hand. Moreover, the last digit of the date,
"4," has been altered, perhaps from "0." It is
not impossible that this was issued in London in 1644 from a plate the artist left
behind when he went to Antwerp that year.

Sir Anthony Van Dyck

Etching (P.1393; second state of three)
1644
135 × 115; 5¼ × 4½

Robert J. D. Harding

This copies Van Dyck's *Self-Portrait with the Sunflower* of c. 1633, the best known version of which is in the collection of the Duke of Westminster. The print is dedicated to John Evelyn by Hendrick van der Borcht. The sunflower to which Van Dyck points is a symbol of art, and he raises an elaborate gold chain, another symbol of *Pittura*.

Hollar's insistent, even stubborn, denial of the baroque is particularly evident in this print. The elegant tilt of Van Dyck's head in the original, has here been straightened up to a more erect posture, and the curve of his back has been eliminated by the encroaching edge of the left border. The distinctive and unusual oblong format has been converted into a square one, and Hollar has altered the leaves of the sunflower, which now touch the edge as a single mass rather than as three separate leaves divided by patches of sky. The design thus becomes more austere and linear, and the relation of the pose to the format and its dimensions is radically different.

Van Dyck died in 1641, and it is difficult to believe that he would have sanctioned Hollar's editing of his design. However, it appears to have been Hollar's interpretation of the painting, rather than the original, that influenced Sir Peter Lely and Robert Walker in their self-portraits.[1]

1. Lindsay Stainton and Christopher White, *Drawing in England from Hilliard to Hogarth* (London: British Museum, 1987), 890.

DNO: IOHANNI EVELINO GENE. ANGLO, ARTIS PICTVræ Amatori & Admiratori Maximo, Amico & Patrono suo fidelissimo &c. Hanc Dñi Anthony van Dyck, Equitis Effigiem, manu eius propria delineatam & a Wenceslao Hollar Bohemo, in hac forma aqua forti æri insculptam, Observantiæ ergo, Henric van der Borcht iun: D.D.D. A° 1644.

Ant: van dyck pinxit   Web Hollar fecit Londini

Philippus Le Roy

SIR ANTHONY VAN DYCK (1599–1641)

Philip, Baron Le Roy, Lord of Ravels

Etching (Hollstein 19; Mauquoy-Hendrickx 18, first
state of eight)
243 × 156; 9½ × 6⅛

Duke of Devonshire and the Trustees of the
Chatsworth Settlement

In this early state the print is in pure etching
and the work confined to the head and
shoulders. Later, for its publication in
Antwerp in *Iconographie,* it was worked up
and finished in engraving by another hand.
Hollar must have known these brilliant
etched studies by Van Dyck representing
contemporary Flemish artists, but his work
in portraiture shows scant reaction to their
baroque dynamism, remaining largely static
and unruffled.

JAN LIEVENS (1607–1674)

Portrait of an Old Man, Possibly Robert South

Etching (Hollstein 28; first state of three)
286 × 220; 11¼ × 8½

Private collection

Two early impressions of this etching, at
Rotterdam and Vienna, bear old ink inscrip-
tions identifying the sitter as the English-
man Robert South, aged 112. Another, in
Munich, identifies the sitter as Lord Digby.
Whatever the truth of the matter, it seems
possible that this wonderfully direct and free
etching was made in England, where Jan
Lievens worked between 1632 and 1635.
However, Clifford Ackley[1] gives it to
Lievens' Antwerp period (1635–1644).

Lievens has been overshadowed in his
achievements as a printmaker by Rembrandt, a great friend in his early years. If
indeed this portrait was etched in England,
it would represent one of the summits of the
art in that country.

1. *Printmaking in the Age of Rembrandt* (Boston:
Museum of Fine Arts, 1980), no. 93.

A

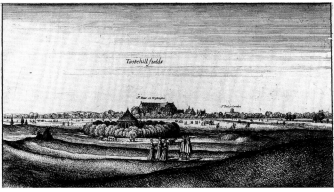

C

B

D

50

English Views

A London, Viewed from Milford
   Stairs
B View of Lambeth from Whitehall Stairs
C Tothill Fields
D Windsor (dated 1644)

Etchings (P.911–P.914)
Each plate: approximately 97 × 173; 3¾ × 6⅞

Yale Center for British Art, Paul Mellon Fund;
B1988.3.1–4

These views are described by Vertue, probably correctly, as a set of four, though the
subjects are not cohesive and the two river

views (P.911 and P.912) could serve as an
independent pair of prints. Most original of
these views is *Tothill Fields,* in which Westminster Abbey is seen beyond open fields
and the foreground is defined by a beautiful
sequence of rolling curved lines.

51

Views in Germany, Holland, and Flanders

Etchings (P.763–P.774; second state of two, with the numbers at lower left)
1642
Each plate: approximately 48 × 168; 1¼ × 6½
Provenance: William Esdaile (L.2617), inscribed by him on verso "1826 Graves sale 12 pes 29+"

Josefowitz Collection

There is no title page—and, according to Pennington, the numeration is not in Hollar's hand—but these twelve plates clearly constitute a series, and one of unusual harmony and beauty. The lines of the water, the banks of earth, and the rigging of the ships seem to flow from one plate to another.

The first nine plates are clearly made from drawings executed in Germany at various times before 1636, while plate 10 is a view of Kampen in Holland seen from across the Dronter Meer. This print is one of the few by Hollar to suggest the miseries of the Thirty Years War, showing a scaffold with dangling remnants of corpses. The last two plates depict Lillo, a part of the outer defenses of Antwerp, and a distant view of Antwerp itself. Unless Hollar had visited Antwerp in 1634, the plates must have been etched in Antwerp after 1644 in the somewhat archaic oblong format that gives cohesion to the set. However, it has been persuasively suggested that a chalk drawing of the Grand Place at Brussels is drawn in a manner commensurate with that in drawings of 1633 and 1636 (Sprinzels 41, 110, no. 348).[1] It is not impossible, therefore, that

Hollar visited Flanders at an earlier date, perhaps 1634.

Plate 2—a view of Strasbourg that is signed, dated, and inscribed "1642. London" —is the only dated print of the set. It suggests that with the loss of his patron Arundel, Hollar was also looking to an overseas market for his prints.

Complete sets of these views are rare. This set is of exceptionally fine quality and uniformity. Five of the set are on paper with an elaborate watermark of either a pot with the letters PRO or a pot with letters PI. Heawood notes the first of these as being a London mark found on sheets documented as 1662. If they were printed as late as that, the plates show remarkably little sign of wear.

1. *Drawings from the Springell Collection*, Sotheby's, London, 30 June 1986, lot 20.

Alburgum in Comitatu Surriæ, vulgo Albury, olim mansio frequens Illustrissimi D.D. Thomæ Howardi Comitis Arundeliæ et Surriæ, &c. Occidentem versus. WHollar fecit.

52

Albury House

Etching (P.954)
130 × 245; 5 × 9½

Robert J. D. Harding

This rare etching is undated, but the phrase in the inscription, *olim mansio frequens* ("formerly the house frequented"), means that it must have been etched after Arundel departed England in 1642. Albury House was Arundel's country residence in Surrey, a place to which he became more and more attached in his old age. The rambling Elizabethan structure was referred to wistfully by Arundel, eking out his last days in Padua, as "my poore little Cottage." He took a great interest in gardening and in improving the estate, and Hollar's etching, showing the distant deer park and a large coach and horsemen arriving at the house, evokes the calm and ordered ambience that was so congenial to him in his troubled old age.

A

B

C

53

The Earl of Arundel on Horseback

A   THIRD STATE

Etching (P.1352; third state of six, still with the portrait head of Arundel)
1639
280 × 220; 11 × 8⅝

Robert J. D. Harding

B   FOURTH STATE

Etching (P.1352; fourth state, with Arundel's head erased from the plate and replaced by that of Fairfax)
1639
280 × 220; 11 × 8⅝

C   SIXTH STATE

Etching (P.1352; sixth and final state, with the head of Fairfax erased and replaced by that of Oliver Cromwell)
1639
280 × 220; 11 × 8⅝

Private collection

This reusing of old plates by erasing the head of one sitter and replacing it with another more who was politically favored or newsworthy is typical of the hurried, unscrupulous world of London print publishing during the Civil War. The first intention of Hollar's plate was to celebrate Arundel's excursion to Scotland in 1637 at the head of an English army—an inglorious episode. Evidently this plate was left behind by the artist when he went to Antwerp in 1644.

The head of Fairfax in the fourth state is very poorly engraved by another hand, presumably a hack hired by Thomas Hind, the publisher of this state. Fairfax was a parliamentarian general, who thus steps, literally, into the shoes of the royalist Arundel. In the final state the plate is worn to a shadow by repeated use. It was published by Peter Stent, an eager purveyor of second- and third-hand plates.

54

Nathaniel Nye, aged 20

Etching (P.1475; first state of two)
1644
139 × 93; 5½ × 3¾
Provenance: P. J. Mariette (L.1788) inscribed and dated
1668 on verso

Richard Godfrey

Nye was a mathematician whose book *The Art of Gunnery* was published in 1647. This portrait, which is one of Hollar's successful, was used as the frontispiece. A second edition was published in 1670. It is likely, however, that the portrait was first intended as a separate plate. Presumably Nye purchased the plate, as he was able to use it in 1647, when Hollar was in Antwerp.

Royal Exchange

Etching (P.1036; second state of three)
1644
295 × 394; 11⅝ × 15½

Dr. and Mrs. Howard A. Fox

The Royal Exchange was modeled on the Bourse in Antwerp and built in 1566 and 1567 by Sir Thomas Gresham (whose portrait in a circle hangs from the cartouche), and was the center of British commercial activity. Here it is thronged by a diverse crowd that includes two Muscovites in fur hats at the left. Also in the foreground at the left is a woman selling broadsides. In the niches above the arches on the right are statues of English monarchs, from Edward the Confessor to Charles I, with three vacant niches. The statue of Charles I was torn down after his execution in 1649. The Exchange was gutted in the Great Fire, and Hollar's print was thus given a new lease of life as the best record of the building, being reissued in 1668.

56

Civilis Seditio

Etching (P. 481)
1643
70 × 110; 2¾ × 4¼

Private collection

This satire on the Civil War depicts an *amphisbaena* (a double-headed snake) crawling in the desert. Behind are the Sphinx and a number of pyramids. This telling linear design is based on an early crude broadside woodcut showing that "if one draw too hard one way, and the other another, the whole Common-Wealth must be in danger to be pull'd in sunder."[1]

1. F. G. Stephens and Dorothy George, *Catalogue of Political and Personal Satires* (London: British Museum, 1870), 314.

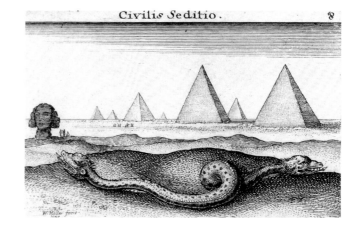

57

En Surculus Arbor

Etching (P.480; second state of two, with the verses below cut off)
1641
125 × 196; 5 × 7½

Private collection

Two lions rear up on their hind legs and grasp the stem of an orange tree as a number of ships sail on the sea beyond. This is an allegory on the dynastic marriage between Mary, the daughter of Charles I, and William, the son of Frederick, Prince of Orange. This union of the English and Dutch Royal Houses allowed Dutch neutrality in the civil war and also resulted in the future ascent to the English throne of William III.

A Comparison of the English and Bohemian Civil Wars

Etching (P.543)

303 × 375; 11⅞ × 14¾

British Museum, London; Mn 3–52

This intensely personal print reflects calmly on the artist's misfortune on leaving the civil strife of Bohemia and the Continent for the peaceful haven of England, only to experience that country's doleful descent into civil war.

A map of England is shown at the left with various battles raging, while on the right is a view of Prague with the Battle of the White Mountain of 1620. The small scenes in compartments at the sides show different events from both conflicts, the dating of which places the print some time after 1642. The design is of particular sophistication, the cartographic depiction of England contrasting with the naturalistic perspective of the hills of Bohemia. Skillfully deployed ornamental forms link the different elements of the design. The lines at the bottom, from Virgil's *Eclogue I*, describe the invasion of pastoral felicity by civil war.

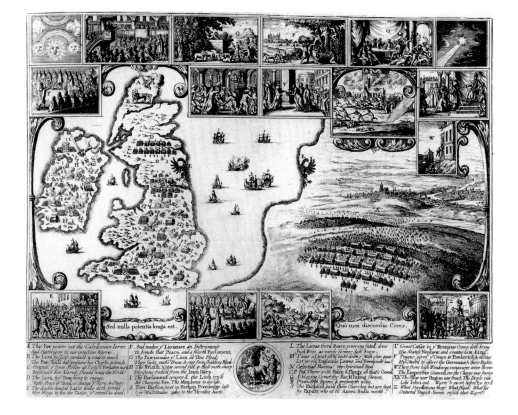

59

Views of Albury

Etchings (P.938, P.939, P.941, and P.942) from the set of six (P.937–P.942)
1645
Each plate: approximately 89 × 157; 3½ × 6¼

Dr. and Mrs. Howard A. Fox

Albury was Arundel's country retreat in Surrey. Arundel, in desolate exile in Padua at the end of his life, wrote longingly of "or poore Cottage at Alleberrye where I hope to be ere long & end my days there." John Evelyn visited the Arundel in Padua and was given a sheaf of "Remembrances," including the instruction that "I desire that Daniel House give me a particular accounte howe my water & all thinges are at Albury. & that he will have great care that agaynest the Gallery & House, store of Roses Cherimine wodbines & ye like sweetes be plantes." Aubrey describes how Arundel "had many Grotts about his house, cutt in the Sandy sides of hills, wherein he delighted to sit and discourse." The rector at Albury, whose church is visible in a number of the views, was the famous mathematician William Oughtred (fig. 13), to whom Arundel was devoted. They spent many hours in discourse, both in the "Grotts" (where they were once nearly killed by a landfall), and while sitting placidly in a boat in the middle of the lake.

On the evidence of these prints, which were etched in Antwerp from drawings made in England, Hollar was very familiar with the country around Albury. The well-clad group who perambulates the slopes in two of the prints is surely intended to represent Arundel and his family. These idyllic views, full of peace and restful contentment, are among Hollar's most beautiful landscapes, given the piquancy of nostalgia by their retrospective execution. Even the lettering is fitted to the sky as if it belongs there, like the birds circling the church steeple.

60

Arundel House from the North

Etching (P.1034)
1649
85 × 195; 3 × 7½

Arundel House from the South

Etching (P.1035)
1646
85 × 195; 3 × 7½

Private collection

Hollar has inadvertently reversed his compass points, the north and south directions being transposed from one print to another. The first shows the courtyard of Arundel House, a somewhat ramshackle assemblage of inelegant wooden houses, with a bustle of horsemen and coaches and a distant view of Lambeth marshes. The buildings were probably for the use of retainers rather than members of the Arundel family.

The second print shows another view of the courtyard, the house at the left being continuous to that at the right of P.1034. At the right is a small building with a skylight above and two unidentifiable pictures (one framed) propped up on the wall outside. It

is perfectly possible that this was Hollar's studio and that the two gentleman who knock at the door have delivered paintings for him to copy.

Both prints are inscribed "Adam. A. Bierling delin. W. Hollar fecit. 1646." This remains utterly baffling. Nothing is known of Bierling as an artist nor of his presence in England. We know him solely as the Antwerp publisher of a number of Hollar plates, especially those of subjects by Holbein. The composition and execution of the plates is entirely in Hollar's spirit, and the subjects very personal to him. Yet the inscription, which appears to be etched in Hollar's hand, is undeniable.

61

London Views

A WESTMINSTER FROM THE RIVER
B LAMBETH PALACE FROM THE RIVER
C WHITEHALL FROM THE RIVER
D WESTMINSTER HALL

Etchings (P.1037–P.1040; all second state of three with numbers)
1647
Each plate: approximately 150 × 325; 5¾ × 12½

Private collection

Westminster from the River shows, from a midriver vantage point, the Parliament House, Parliament Hall, and the Abbey. A number of boats disgorge their passengers at Westminster Steps at the center.

Lambeth Palace from the River is a view from midriver of Lambeth Palace, the official residence of the archbishops of Canterbury, chief prelates of the Church of England. At right, beneath a clump of trees, emerges the archbishop, probably the controversial William Laud, whose train is born by attendants. A number of common folk make obeisance before him.

Whitehall from the River is a view, from across the river at Lambeth marshes, of the great Banqueting House at Whitehall. The importance and dominating position of this great building is emphasized by its appearance in a number of Hollar etchings. This etching is a particularly noble design, its elements disposed with great clarity and simplicity. Hollar's treatment of the sky and water is particularly formalized.

In *Westminster Hall* numerous coaches are drawn up in the square to the north part of the Hall, which is seen on the left of the print. This medieval building is used for state occasions, including the lying-in-state of Winston Churchill in 1964.

This set of prints was etched in Antwerp, evidently from drawings made in London. They constitute a coherent group of four, but the numbers are misleading and probably added later.

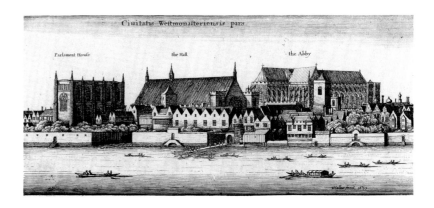

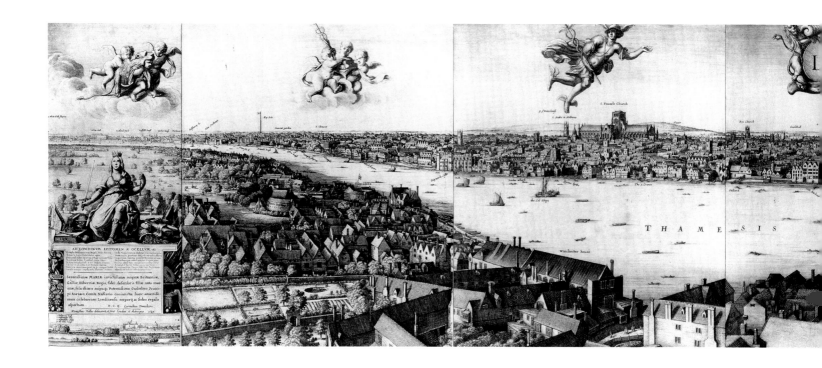

62

The Long View of London from Bankside

Etching (P.1014), printed from six plates
1647
2838 × 2364; 108 × 90
Each plate: approximately 473 × 394; 18⅝ × 15½

British Museum, London; 1864-6-11-334/a

Published in Amsterdam in 1647, the plates were executed from drawings made earlier in London. This is one of Hollar's masterpieces, and one of the greatest of all panoramic prints, supplanting a 1616 panorama of London by Claesz Janz Visscher. The precision and disposition of the great expanse of buildings is majestic, only slightly diminished by the somewhat doughy figures in the sky. Allegorical figures of London and the Thames are placed at the left and right of the composition, respectively.

Hollar based the view on drawings made from the tower of St. Mary Overy, Southwark. The buildings are carefully labeled, Hollar's imperfect English being evident in the misspelling of "S. Pauwls Church."

However, Hollar had copied some of the labels from Visscher's 1616 panorama, with consequent misunderstandings; thus, the circular building at the left called the Globe is in fact the Hope Theatre, replacing the bear-baiting building which was demolished in 1614, and the larger circular building labeled "Beere bayting" is in fact the second Globe Theatre of 1614, replacing Shakespeare's theatre which burned in 1613.

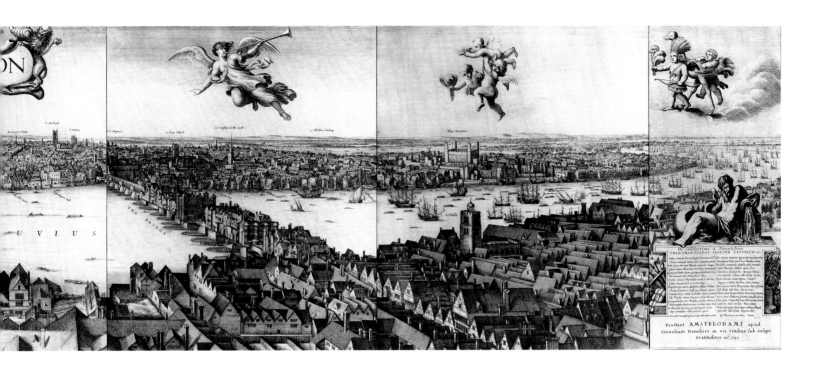

De Celeberrima & Florentissima
TRINOBANTIADOS AUGUSTÆ CIVITATE

Proſtant AMSTELODAMI apud
Cornelium Danckers in via vitulina ſub inſigni
Gratitudines Aᵒ 1647

63

A View of the East Part of Southwark, Looking Towards Greenwich

Pen and brown ink over black chalk on joined
sheets of paper
140 × 308; 5½ × 12⅛

Yale Center for British Art, Paul Mellon
Collection; B1977.14.4464

This is a study made from the tower of St. Mary Overy, Southwark, for the right-hand portion of *The Long View of London from Bankside.* However, comparison with the etching shows many changes in details, such as the tower of St. Olafe's on the riverbank. The whole sweep of the design and the extent of the river are also greatly enhanced in the finished print though merely indicated in the drawing. Finally, in the print the structure of the myriad rooftops becomes, if anything, even more sharp and schematized.

It is to be presumed that the graphite drawing was made from life and that the pen outlines were added in the studio, and that many more such studies must have existed.

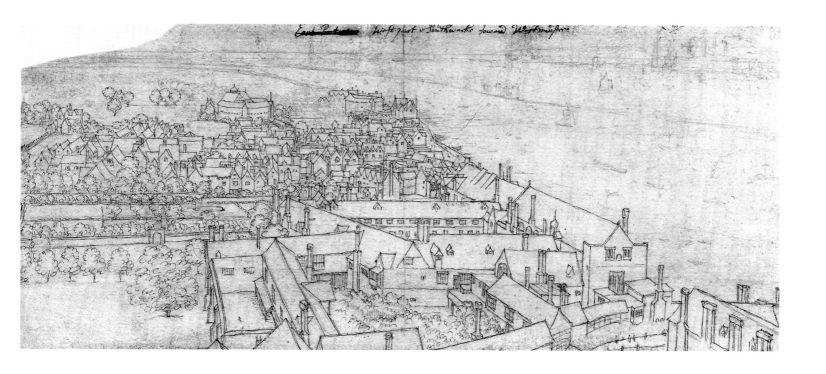

64

A View from St. Mary's, Southwark, Looking Towards Westminster

Pen and black ink over graphite on two joined sheets
127 × 306; 5 × 12⅟₁₆

Yale Center for British Art, Paul Mellon
Collection; B1977.14.5548

A study for the central-left portion of *The Long View of London from Bankside.* The far side of the Thames, with Old St. Paul's at the right, is only indicated. In the finished print Hollar considerably altered the perspectival scheme and many of the details so that the structures could conform with the logic of the long format and design. The long medieval house at the right is Winchester House, with its extensive gardens (built over in 1663).

65

Designs for Daggers and Scabbards

Etching (P.2596; second state of two)
1644
156 × 105; 6⅛ × 4¼

Robert J. D. Harding

Holbein's original drawings for this and other dagger and scabbard designs etched by Hollar are now lost. It is possible that Hollar was arranging on one sheet four small separate drawings by Holbein, to form a more interesting design. The emphasis of the edges and the lucid definition of the white spaces between the objects are characteristic of Hollar.

Although this reproduces a drawing in the Arundel collection, the address of Henricus van der Borcht suggests that the etching was published in Antwerp.

66

Five Grotesque Old Men

Etching (P.1609)
1646
245 × 186; 9¾ × 7¼

Metropolitan Museum of Art, New York;
26.72.107

Hollar etched this design in Antwerp, probably from a drawing made in England from Leonardo's original, which was then in the Arundel collection and is now at the Royal Library, Windsor Castle. This is the most striking and resolved of Leonardo's caricatures, and Hollar was at pains to capture not merely the spirit of the drawing but its exact appearance, line by line. He has slightly reduced its dimensions by about 30mm vertically and 20mm horizontally, however.

Leonardo's drawings of grotesque heads are not in the strict sense caricatures; nonetheless, through the intermediary of Hollar's prints, they exerted enormous influence on the development of the caricature in England in the eighteenth century.

67

A Young Man with a Hideous Old Woman

Etching (P.1604)
1646
170 × 131; 6⅝ × 5⅛

Metropolitan Museum of Art, New York;
17.50.18.162

Hollar's model was a now lost drawing in the Arundel collection. It was then attributed to Leonardo da Vinci but more likely was by a close imitator. This particular impression is, most unusually, printed on mauve paper. It is not known if the print reverses the drawing, but, atypically, no counterproofs are recorded by Pennington, and until one is located there remains a possibility that the print and drawing are in the same direction and that the present impression is intended as a facsimile. It strongly suggests the appearance of a Leonardesque sheet in silverpoint or metalpoint on prepared colored paper.

See plate 8

68

Saint Barbara

Etching (P.176)
1647
204 × 127; 8 × 5

Robert J. D. Harding

This reproduces a drawing by Holbein once in the Arundel collection but no longer preserved. A number of early drawings made by Holbein in Basel represent fashionable ladies of that city. They are secular in type, and even somewhat erotic in posture. Hollar was probably working from a study made in London from Holbein's original. His veracity to that model is impossible to verify, but it may be observed that the river landscape is characteristic of Hollar's early views of the Rhine and very unlike any drawings known by Holbein. The formalized clouds are purely Hollarean, and the etcher may have been attempting to give greater pictorial interest to the design.

The identification of the figure as St. Barbara is uncertain, as, indeed, is the very existence of such a saint. Her customary emblem of a tower may be intended by the two small towers on the mountainous river bank at the left.

LATONA

Dr Henrico van der Borcht seniori omnium Raritatum & Elegantiarum Amatori & Collectori maximo, D.D: Wenceslaus Hollar A.º 1649

Elsheimer inventi. Wenceslaus Hollar fecit aqua forti, ex Collectione Arundeliana. 1644.

69

Latona

Etching (P.272)
1649
173 × 237; 6¼ × 9⅜

Frank W. Raysor II

The story of Latona, from Ovid's *Metamorphoses,* resembles that of Ceres and Stellio. Latona begged three peasants for water to slake her thirst and that of her two children, Apollo and Diana. They refused churlishly, and in her anger Latona transformed them into frogs.

The painting, which is recorded as being in Arundel's collection, was lost for many years, but it reappeared in 1980 when it was identified by Keith Andrews as Adam Elsheimer's original. Hollar's print is almost exactly the same size as the painting and in reverse direction. The painting is now much damaged, but it is still apparent that Hollar made significant changes in the composition. In the painting the foreground is filled by a curving bank of earth culminating in a tree trunk at the right. This is eliminated by Hollar, who represents the water as a continuous horizontal mass with the straight-edged lines running parallel to the lower border line. This radically changes the whole rhythmic structure of the design.

A

70

Ceres and Stellio

A ETCHING

Etching (P.273)
1646
300 × 230; 11¾ × 9

Dr. and Mrs. Howard A. Fox

B COUNTERPROOF

Counterproof of P.273
1646
300 × 230; 11¾ × 9

Yale University Art Gallery; 1927.106

Hollar was not copying Adam Elsheimer's original painting, which is now lost, but the reproductive engraving by Hendrick Goudt, made in Rome in 1610. Goudt's highly wrought engravings after Elsheimer's nocturnal scenes were widely circulated and very influential, Jacques Callot and Abraham Bosse being but two artists who profited from their example. Hollar has even copied Goudt's verses beneath the design, but he has not acknowledged the Dutch engraver as his source. Goudt was still alive when Hollar etched this plate. He died in Utrecht in 1648.

In Ovid's *Metamorphoses,* the goddess Ceres, parched with thirst, asked for a drink of water from an old peasant woman. So thirstily did she drink that the peasant woman's son laughed aloud, and, for his pains, was turned into a lizard by the goddess.

Hollar's etching is in reverse to Goudt's print, which in its turn was almost certainly in reverse to Elsheimer's painting, since his prints from surviving paintings are never in the correct sense.

By its nature a print is always a mirror

Dum frugum genitrix, tædas accendit in Ætna.
Et tete natam quærit in Orbe suam.
Victa siti conspexit anum, Lymphamque rogavit.
Orante Lympham Rustica dulce dedit.

Dum bibit acceptum, risit puer improbus illam.
Nec satis hoc, quidam dixerat ille Deam.
Rudentem Liquida fertur sparsisse polenta
fuissee, sed iam stellis factus erat.

A. Elsheimer pinxit.   W. Hollar fecit aqua forti
                                                                                                                              1646

B

image of the matrix from which it is printed. This can sometimes result in unbalanced compositions, though with experience printmakers learn to gauge the effect of reversal or develop a means of transferring their design onto the plate in such a way that it will print in the correct sense to their original. Thus Hollar's topographical views preserve the correct sense of the landscape while his copies of paintings and drawings, with rare exceptions (such as the *Wilton Diptych*), do not. In the latter category Hollar therefore made extensive use of counterproofs to serve both as a technical aid and, more important, as an accurate record of the composition that he was copying.

A counterproof is easily made by attaching a dampened fresh sheet of paper to a freshly printed impression and running it through the press again. The resulting impression, though sometimes pale, brings the composition back to its original sense. Besides the outstanding counterproof at Yale, there are also examples at Windsor and the Fitzwilliam Museum, Cambridge, and other subjects are known in multiple examples. There can be no doubt that these were marketable items sought out by discerning collectors. Rembrandt also made extensive use of counterproofs, sometimes employing them to recapture the correct topographical sense of a landscape (there are six recorded counterproofs of the *Goldweigher's Field*, for example), or to provide an alternative to a design that he felt had suffered by reversal. There are, for instance, at least seven known counterproofs of *Abraham's Sacrifice*.

71

Pallas

Etching (P.270)
1646
92 × 147; 3⅝ × 5¾

Frank W. Raysor II

This etching was copied from a tiny painting by Adam Elsheimer that once was
in the Arundel collection and now is in the
Fitzwilliam Museum, Cambridge. Elsheimer's small, intensely atmospheric paintings
were much prized by Arundel and relished
by Hollar, who developed an elaborate finished technique to suggest their dimly lit
interiors and shady forests. His etchings
after Elsheimer are among the most personal and interesting of all his copies.

72

Self-Portrait in an Oval

Etching (P.1420; first state of eight)
1647
128 × 91; 5 × 3⅝

Dr. and Mrs. Howard A. Fox

Hollar depicts himself in a somewhat
melancholic vein, in contrast to the cheery
mood of the Meyssens portrait (no. 75).
Beneath the oval he represents his coat of
arms. In the second state this was changed
to the coat of arms of his father, an unexpected alteration given his clear antipathy to
his parent, who had opposed his chosen
career as an artist.

A Twenty-Three-Year-Old Virginian Algonquian

Etching (P.2009; first state of two)
1645
104 × 77; 4⅛ × 3
Provenance: William Young Ottley (L.2662, L.2665)

Dr. and Mrs. Howard A. Fox

This print is inscribed "W. Hollar ad vivum—delin: et fecit" to make it clear that this is a portrait made from life, with due attention paid to the details of the sitter's tattoos, head circlet of teeth, and necklace of small beads and shells. It is apparently the first portrait print, made from life, of a Native American. The inscription also implies that the drawing was made in Antwerp, though it is not impossible that Hollar was working from a study made earlier in England. The Virginia Company had been founded in 1606, and in 1616 a group of Virginia natives was brought to England by Sir Thomas Dale. Perhaps this records another such visit.

In 1645 the Virginia Algonquians were much harassed by English colonists, who were usurping their territories. (The Algonquians are not to be confused with the Algonquins, a more warlike tribe from the Hudson Bay region.) That same year Hollar also etched the studies *A Turk's Head* (P.2010) and *A Young Negress* (P.2006), showing an interest in diverse racial types. The works do not constitute a set, however.

74

Young Woman with Side-Curls

Etching (P.1716)
1645
85 × 64; 3⅓ × 2½

Young Woman with Side-Curls; back view

Etching (P.1717)
1645
85 × 59; 3⅓ × 2¼

Dr. and Mrs. Howard A. Fox

Parthey's suggestion that this pair of studies represents Hollar's first wife is unsupported by any evidence save the intimate and loving quality of its observation. It should perhaps be described as a pair of studies of a girl's hair, since that is where the artist's interest lay. Pennington rejects Parthey's identification and notes that the second plate is dated 1645, when the artist was in Antwerp, and that the "obviously Dutch" costume precludes an identification with Mrs. Hollar. There is no evidence that she did not accompany Hollar on his travels, however, and the simple costume could equally be English, Hollar making use of an earlier drawing. Pennington further notes incorrectly that the original drawing is at Prague and that preliminary sketches for both plates were in the Springell collection. This presumably refers to the single sheet with two studies that was sold in the Springell sale.[1] In my opinion those studies have absolutely no connection with the two etchings beyond a coincidental (and slight) similarity of pose.

These arguments apart, the etchings are among the most beautiful of Hollar's work, poems to femininity that find their counterparts in much Caroline verse.

1. Sotheby's, London, 30 June 1985, lot 15.

Wenceslaus Hollar

Etching (P.1419; second state of five)
159 × 114; 6½ × 4½
Provenance: Hermann Weber (L. 1383)

Frank W. Raysor II

This work was etched by Hollar in Antwerp from a painting or grisaille made by Jan Meyssens, who also published the print in 1649 as part of a series of portraits of artists. His portrait of Hollar's friend Hendrick van der Borcht belongs to the same series. The biographical details given in French in the inscription space are our most reliable source for the basic facts of Hollar's career, and they were presumably provided by the artist himself.

> WENCESLAUS HOLLAR: Gentilhomme ne a Prage l'an 1607, a este de nature fort inclin pr l'art de meniature principale-ment pour esclaircir, mais beaucoup retarde par son pere, l'an 1627, il est party de Prage aijant dmeure en divers lieux en Allemagne,il c est addonne pour peu de temps a esclaircir et aplicquer leau forte, estant party de Coloigne avec le Comte d'Arondel vers Vienne et dillec par Prage vers Angleterre, ou aijant este serviteur domestique du Duc de lorck, il s'est retire de la cause de la guerre a Anvers ou il reside encores.

The artist is shown half-length with a window to his right beyond which is a view of a city with a large church on the skyline. This has sometimes been identified with the cathedral of St. Vitus in Prague, but it does not resemble it. He is holding a copper plate of *St. Catherine* (P.177), a plate he etched from a painting attributed to Raphael in the Arundel collection that now is lost. On the table before him are numerous tools and materials, including a bottle of acid with a burin beside it, compasses, etching needles, and set squares. The face is rather awk-wardly worked, but bears a marked resem-blance to the *Laughing Self-Portrait* from the *Reisbuchlein* (no. 13).

A *Portrait of an Unknown Architect* by Sebastian Bourdon (Collection, Duke of Buccleuch, Boughton) has been identified by Michael Jaffé as a portrait of Hollar.[1] This is entirely improbable. The resemblance to the portrait is only slight, and what Jaffé identifies as a "mid-line cyst" beneath the sitter's lower lip is merely the small imperial beard sported by innumerable sitters of the period. There is not a scrap of evidence that Hollar ever visited France, let alone in 1657, when he was busy with the plates for Dug-dale's *St. Paul's Cathedral.* It is surely incon-ceivable that he should have visited France and not left us with a single print or draw-ing of a French subject.

1. Tessa Murdoch, ed., *Boughton House: The English Versailles* (London, 1992), 77, 218, pl. 42.

Henry Van der Borcht the Younger

Etching (P.1365; second state of five)
1648
165 × 115; 6½ × 4½
Provenance: Francis Springell

Robert J. D. Harding

Van der Borcht (1614–1654) was a painter and occasional etcher employed by Arundel in Cologne at the same time as Hollar. Arundel sent Van der Borcht to Italy to acquire the rudiments of connoisseurship from Arundel's agent, William Petty. He traveled to Italy with William Harvey, and Arundel wrote to Petty that he had "sent with the Doctor Hervey a youth called Henry van de Burg, son of a painter in Frankfurt, to attend you, and return hither with you. He is a very honest youth, and loves all matters of art dearly." He was Hollar's colleague at Arundel House from 1637, but he seems to have traveled to Antwerp with Arundel's collection in 1642. His responsibilities appear to have been mainly curatorial, though he did etch a few plates after drawings in the collection.

Hollar's etching portrays Van der Borcht holding an album open at a page with a design then attributed to Raphael but unlikely to have been by him. This is from a series of portraits painted and published in Antwerp by Meyssens that included a portrait of Hollar.

HENRY VAN DER BORCHT PEINCTRE,
Né a Franckendael au Palatinat, et a cause de la Guerre venu a Franckfort, eu l an 1636 paſſant le Comte d'Arondell Voyagant vers l'Empereur, l'emmena et de la l'enuoya en Italie Ches M' Peti le quel amaſſa l'Art Pour le dit Comte, de la Paſſant auec l'art en Angleterre il l a garde Juſques au deces du Comte il eſt Seruiteur du Prince de Galles,

Iohann: Meyſſens pinxit et excudit,   W: Hollar fecit, 1648,

Women's Heads in Circles

Etchings (P.1932–P.1944 from the series of thirty-seven plates P.1908–P.1944)
1642–1647
Each plate: approximately 100 × 95; 4 × 3¾

Private collection

It seems likely that this series was never completed, since there is no title page, and thirty-seven is an unbalanced number. Their purpose seems in general to be the illustration of fashion rather than portraiture, although likenesses in some of the faces should not to be ruled out. The series was begun in London and continued in Antwerp. One of the plates, P.1927 (not exhibited) was copied from a miniature or portrait drawing by John Hoskins. Hollar shaded the edges of the oval designs to leave patches of light behind the heads, creating a brilliant effect.

A Young Man Playing a Lute

Etching (P.1698a)
185 × 130; 7¼ × 5 (trimmed within the platemark)

Private collection

This beautiful etching is a working proof of
great rarity, touched in and around the face
with pale gray wash and light white bodycolor, presumably to indicate changes to be
made in the succeeding state. This previously unrecorded impression is only the second known, the other being in the British
Museum.

The identity of the rather melancholy
youth, who plucks at a double-headed
theorbo lute, is not known. Through the
window can be seen a tower and a number
of ships, one of which flies the St. George's
flag. The stretch of shoreline and the ships
suggest a foreign location, and the flag of St.
George was flown by English navy vessels
between the death of Charles I and the commencement of the Protectorate of Oliver
Cromwell.

Working proofs by Hollar are scarcely to
be found. The rarity of the present subject is
not to be explained, but one possibility must
be that an accident happened to the plate
during its execution. The calm stillness of
the work and the motif of a lute player are
reminiscent of the paintings of Gerard Ter-
borch, one of whose portraits Hollar etched.

79

Charles I

Etching (P.1432; first state of three)
1649
152 × 105; 6 × 4⅛

Dr. and Mrs. Howard A. Fox

This was etched as a memorial portrait in
the year of the king's execution. The place of
his death, the Banqueting House, is shown
at the right behind his shoulder, and Westminster Abbey and the Parliament buildings
can be seen at the left. The figure is based
generally on originals by Van Dyck, but the
background, suggesting the past glories of
the monarch, is Hollar's invention.

Serenissimus Princeps, Carolus D:G: Angliæ,
Scotiæ, & Hiberniæ, REX, etc. &c

Ant: van Dyck. pinxit.   W: Hollar fecit, 1649

80

Charles II

Etching (P.1442; second state of seven)
1649
254 × 185; 10 × 7¼

Metropolitan Museum of Art, New York,
bequest of Susan Dwight Bliss, 1967; 67.630.87

Etched by Hollar in Antwerp after an original by Van Dyck. It was commissioned for
the large set of prints engraved after Van
Dyck originals entitled *Iconographie.* In the
background can be seen the Banqueting
House, one of Hollar's favorite subjects. His
handling of detail is fine, but baroque swag-
ger is notable by its absence.

CAROLVS II. D.G: MAGNÆ BRITANNIÆ FRA.ᵗⁱᵉ et HIBERNIÆ REX, etc. natus A° 1630

Hanc Maiestatis suæ Effigiem ab Antonio van Dycke Equite sic. depictam,   Humillimus Cliens Wenceslaus Hollar Boh:
v. Aqua forti æri insculpsit   Anno 1649.

Ant. van Dycke pinxit.   W. Hollar fecit, et exc.

Naues Mercatoriæ Hollandicæ per Indias Occidentales

81

Dutch West Indiaman

Etchings (P.1265; first and second states of two)
1647
145 × 236; 5¼ × 9¼

Dr. and Mrs. Howard A. Fox

This etching and the one that follows are
from the series *Dutch Ships* (P.1261–
P.1272), published in Antwerp in 1647. Most
of these prints were probably based on
drawings Hollar made in Holland in 1634.
This example is notable for the dramatic
and highly original viewpoint, which creates
a striking architectonic design.

82

Warship

Etching (P.1280)
148 × 217; 5¾ × 8½

Dr. and Mrs. Howard A. Fox

This vessel is a three-masted man-of-war,
with a single gun deck, depicted in rapid
motion. In the background two ships are
engaging each other. Although Hollar delighted in depicting ships in full sail, his
most important contribution to marine art
lay in his studies of ships in harbor.

83

Strasbourg Cathedral

Etching (P.892)
1645
222 × 181; 8⅝ × 7⅛

Dr. and Mrs. Howard A. Fox

The inscription carefully notes that the
drawing was made from life in Strasbourg in
1630, though it was etched in Antwerp in
1645. This is a particularly notable example
of Hollar utilizing a drawing made years
earlier. This beautifully controlled composition acts as a dress rehearsal for the larger
view of Antwerp Cathedral, published in
1649. Hollar emphasizes the greater mass of
the building by silhouetting it against a clear
sky, the spire rising through high clouds and
nearly touching the upper borderline.

TVRRIS ET ÆDES ECCLESIÆ CATHEDRALIS ARGENTINENSIS.
à Wenceslao Hollar Bohemo, prima ad vivum delineata, et aqua forti æri insculpta. A.º 1630. denuoq, facta Antuerpiæ, A.º 1645.

R.do Admodum Dño D: Adriano Vander Reeft, Ecclesia S: Pauli Ordinis Canonicorum Reg: S: August: Congrega:e Windé Semensis Priori digniſſimo, hanc Monasterij sui Rubræ Vallis Imaginem. Observantiæ ergo D: C:Q. Petrus van Avont,

84

Rothendael Abbey

Etching (P.886; first state of three)
1648
153 × 216; 6 × 8½

Frank W. Raysor II

This plate, etched in Antwerp from a drawing by Petrus van Avont, is of particular delicacy and silvery tone.

85

The Peace of Munster

Etching (P.561; first state of two)
1648
219 × 338; 8⅝ × 13¼
Provenance: Smutny (not in Lugt)

Frank W. Raysor II

The historic Peace of Munster concluded years of struggle between the United Provinces and the Spanish Empire. It recognized the independence of the former and the division of the Netherlands into the predominantly Protestant Holland (the United Provinces) and the predominantly Catholic Belgium. The same treaty also required the closure of the River Scheldt to commerce, thus undermining the prosperity of Antwerp.

Hollar was perhaps present at the scene since he signs the plate "delineauit," but, as noted by Pennington, he also made use of an earlier etching by Pieter van der Borcht in Joan Bochius's *Descriptio publicae gratulationis Spectaculorum in adventu . . . Principis Ernesti* (Antwerp, 1595). As usual Hollar responds with verve to the spectacle of great crowds assembled for a notable event.

86

Antwerp Cathedral

Etching (P.824)
1649
489 × 340; 19¼ × 13⅜

Yale University Art Gallery; 1954.9.6

This is the most ambitious and splendid of Hollar's prints of a single building. The quality of biting to differentiate the architectural details of the cathedral is of great refinement. The closely observed figures and the building seen in *repoussoir* in the foreground at right emphasize the great scale of the structure.

ANTVERPIEN' TVRRIS ECCLESIÆ CATHEDRALIS, BEATISSIMÆ VIRGINIS MARIÆ, DEI-PARÆ, ALTITVD. 451½ PED. INSVPER CRVX 15 PED.
ANTWERPSCHEN TOREN VAND: CATHEDRALE KERCK VAND ALDERHEYLICHSTE MAGET MARIA IS HOOCH 451½ VOET, EN HET CRVYS 15. VOET.
CLOCHER DE L'EGLISE CATHEDRALE D'ANVERS DE LA VIERGE MARIE CONTENANT EN HAVLTEVR 451½ PIEDS. OVLTRE LA CROIX ENCOR 15. PIEDS.

87

A Jay, with a Distant View of the Rhine at Remagen

Etching (P.2159)
1646
94 × 106; 3⅝ × 4⅛

Frank W. Raysor II

The background view is identifiable as the Rhine at Remagen by comparison with a drawing at Prague and a preparatory pencil sketch, dated 1636, in the John Rylands Library sketchbook. Hollar has kept the view in the same direction as the drawing. This is a small but particularly monumental design, in which the drawing and etching of the filigree of the two leaves have been executed with infinite delicacy.

88

A Water-Fowl, with a Distant View of a City

Etching (P.2160)
1646
84 × 114; 3¼ × 4½

Frank W. Raysor II

The background view of houses, spires, and towers invites comparison with the distant views of Amsterdam found in the background of several Rembrandt landscape etchings. It is probable that it is taken from an old sketchbook, now lost, and that it dates from Hollar's period in Holland, the landscape being markedly Dutch in character.

89

The Dead Mole

Etching (P.2106)
1646
70 × 140; 2¾ × 5½

Private collection

This is an unusual instance of Hollar's
obsession with fur. The subject is reminiscent of some of the animals to be found in
Jacob Hoefnagel's *Archetypa Studiaque* (no.
97), though without their quasi-allegorical
intention.

A Study of a Woman in Black, Wearing a Hood

Oil on paper (Croft-Murray and Hulton 43)
187 × 104; 7⅜ × 4⅛
Provenance: Sir Hans Sloane, Bart., by whom
bequeathed to the British Museum in 1753

British Museum, London; 5214–4

This and the following exhibit are the only
oil sketches attributed to Hollar. Sloane
purchased his Hollar collection from the
artist's widow, and without this provenance
it would be difficult to sanction their inclusion in Hollar's ouevre. Indeed, this example, with its mysterious hooded figure
walking away from us, is reminiscent of a
romantic image by some nineteenth-cen-
tury French artist, such as Constantin Guys.
Yet such figures, which tantalize us by turning their backs, are quite common in Hollar's fashion subjects, including the plates of
Aula Veneris. The contours of the figures,
and their costumes, are also typical of the
artist, though the flowing movement of this
figure is unusual. The technique, which is
very accomplished and requires carefully
prepared paper, suggests that the paintings
were executed in Antwerp, where painting
in oil on paper was more common than it
was in England. Examples of this technique
are known, for example, by Rubens and Van
Dyck. In the Sloane catalogue these two
subjects are called "Costume of a German
Lady in Black with Hood On," but the costumes could equally be Flemish, and the
muffs are reminiscent of many such garments depicted by Hollar.

See plate 9

Study of a Woman in Black, Wearing a Wide-Brimmed Hat

Oil on paper (Croft-Murray and Hulton 42)
190 × 110; 7½ × 4¼
Provenance: Sir Hans Sloane, Bart., by whom
bequeathed to the British Museum in 1753

British Museum, London; 5214–3

Hollar uses a subdued yellow to silhouette
the figure, who walks on pavement with
buildings lightly indicated behind. The hat
is not of a type found in any of his
English subjects and is more likely to be a
Flemish fashion.

See plate 10

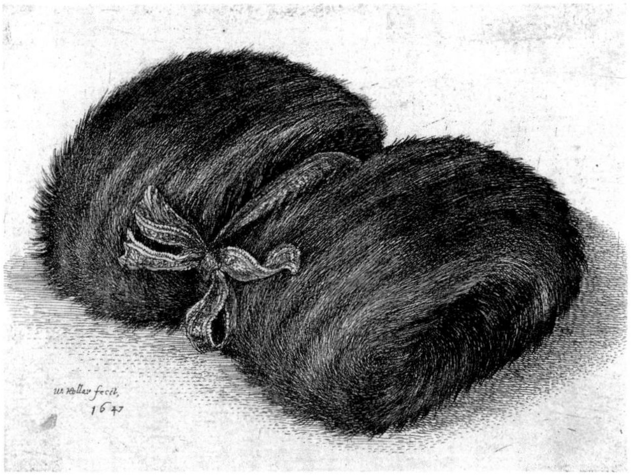

A

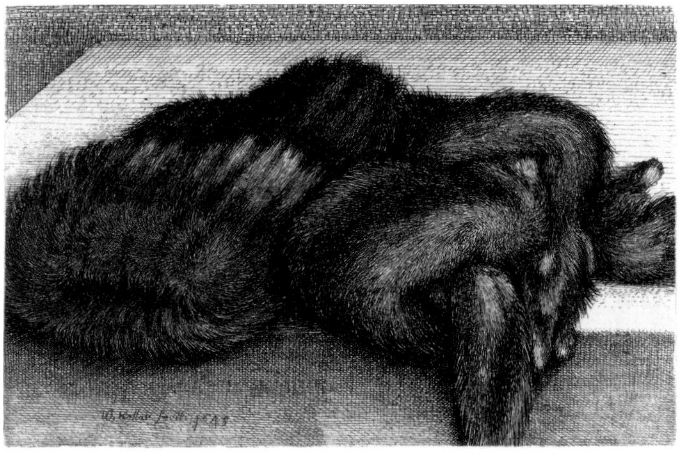

C

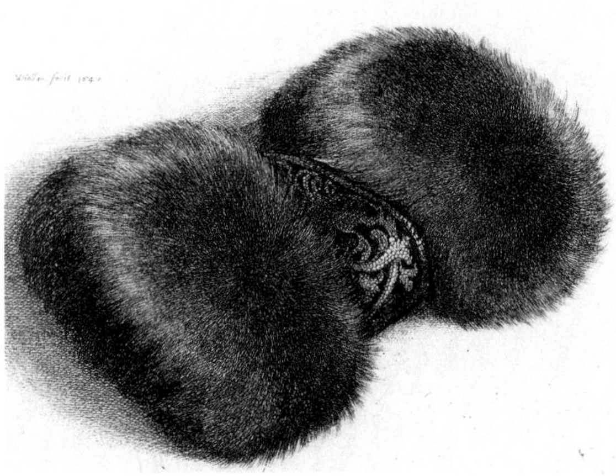

B

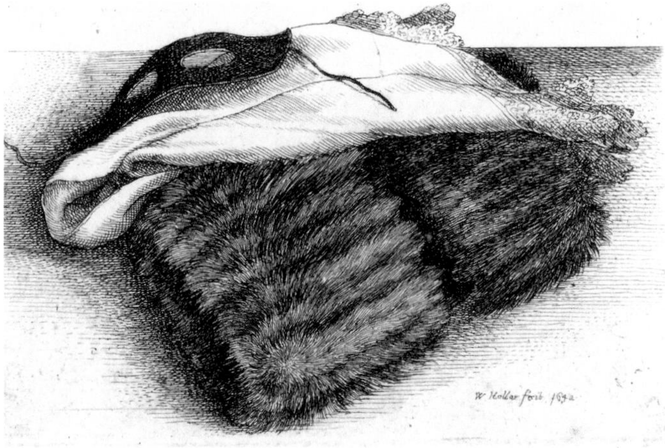

D

92

Muffs

A A Dark Fur Muff
Etching (P.1945)
1647
80 × 111; 3⅛ × 4⅜
Provenance: Alfred Morrison (L.151)

B A Dark Fur Muff
Etching (P.1946)
1647
80 × 112; 3⅛ × 4⅜
Provenance: John Barnard (L. 1419); Julian Marshall (L. 1494); Alfred Morrison (L.151)

C A Dark Fur Muff with Stripes
Etchings (P.1947; first and second states)
1645
82 × 115; 3¼ × 4½
Provenance: Julian Marshall (L. 1494); Alfred Morrison (L.151)

D A Dark Fur Double-Muff
Etching (P.1948)
1642
57 × 93; 2¼ × 3⅝
Provenance: Julian Marshall (L.1494); Alfred Morrison (L.151)

E A Dark Fur Double-Muff
Etching (P.1949)
Undated
57 × 90; 2¼ × 3½
Provenance: Alfred Morrison (L.151)

F A Fur Muff with a Band of Brocade
Etching (P.1950)
1645
94 × 148; 3⅝ × 5¾
Provenance: Doctor Mead (L.1805); Herman Weber (L.1388); Alfred Morrison (L.151)

G A Group of Muffs
Etching (P.1951)
1647
110 × 203; 4 ¼ × 8
Provenance: Julian Marshall (L.1494); Alfred Morrison (L.151)

H A Muff in Five Views
Etching (P.1952)
1640
77 × 128; 3 × 5
Provenance: Julian Marshall (L.1494); Alfred Morrison (L.151)

N. G. Stogdon

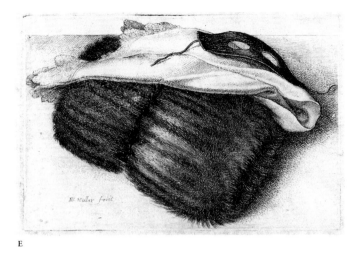

E

G

F

H

These are justly the best loved and admired of all Hollar's prints, and they constitute his most original contribution to the history of printmaking. The closely laid and expertly bitten lines perfectly suggest the softness and warmth of fur, in which Hollar delighted. The delicacy and closeness of the lines is such that they wore quickly and could scarcely be retouched; consequently, fine impressions of them are rare.

Frequently the subject of painters, the depiction of fur had rarely been attempted in prints, and the idea of composing still lifes of these seductive garments was entirely novel. Muffs are depicted in a number of Hollar's fashion prints and are worn by women both of fashion and of sobriety. Yet the appeal of these groups, augmented in some plates by fans, lace, and masks, is undeniably sensuous.

In a number of eighteenth-century English drawings and prints, a fur muff had become an appurtenance suggestive of a streetwalker or woman of easy virtue. A clear example of this is found in Thomas Rowlandson's watercolor *An Old Debaucher* (Yale Center for British Art), a caricature of the Fourth Earl of Queensbury, a well-known lecher. A muff has an even more unequivocal meaning in Dighton's satire of Queensbury, *Old Q-uiz The Old Goat of Piccadilly*, in which Queensbury slips his hand into the muff of a buxom milliner.[1] Yet Hollar's depiction of respectable women wearing muffs in *Ornatus Muliebris* would appear to negate that association in seventeenth-century England, where these works were conceived.

1. Stephens and George, *Satires*, 8867; 1 February 1796.

93

Shells

A Conus imperialis
Etching (P.2195)
98 × 136; 3⅞ × 5⅜

B Fasciolaria tulipa
Etching (P.2200)
92 × 142; 3⅝ × 5⅝

Dr. and Mrs. Howard A. Fox

C Cassis cornuta
Etching (P.2219)
95 × 147; 3¾ × 5¾

D Trochus niloticus
Etching (P.2222)
97 × 145; 3⅞ × 5¾

E Hippopus maculatus
Etching (P.2224)
95 × 149; 3¾ × 5⅞

F Cymbiola nobilis
Etching
95 × 147; 3¾ × 5⅞

Private collection

This celebrated series of prints was unpublished, and its early history is entirely obscure. None of the prints is signed, but the attribution to Hollar has never been challenged, and as early as 1685 (eight years after Hollar's death) five of the prints were copied in Martin Lister's *Historiae conchyliorum* with the acknowledgment "ad exemplar Holleri." Their rarity, even of single examples, has been legendary almost from their conception. The previously unrecorded example F in this exhibition is the only known impression.

Most impressions print with plate-tone and with scratches from the materials used to polish the copper plate—always a sign of early impressions. Such marks, though much appreciated by connoisseurs and often atmospheric in effect, would have

A

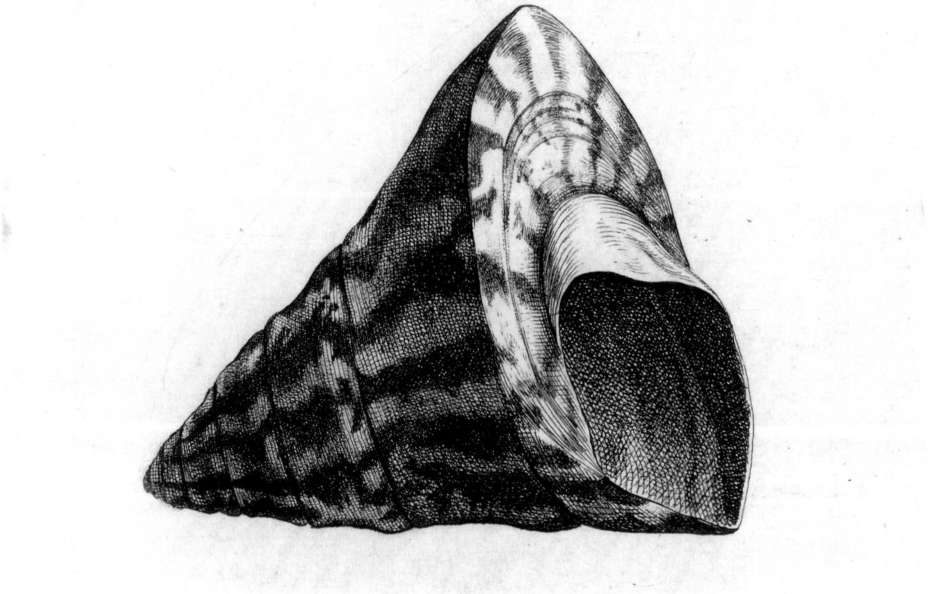

D

E

F

been considered blemishes by Hollar and removed before publication, when he would have added his signature, and, most likely, a description of each shell. It is probably correct, therefore, to consider all known impressions as proofs. Since posthumous impressions are unknown, it must be assumed that the plates were lost or destroyed at an early date. The watermark found on many impressions is that of a Foolscap, a type used regularly in both England and the Netherlands. Technically, the etchings reveal Hollar at the height of his powers, which suggests the Antwerp period as the likeliest time for their execution.

Vertue believed that the actual shells depicted by Hollar came from Arundel's collection, which is possible but unproved. They are, however, presented individually as specimens and without the artifice of presentation that might be considered appropriate for objects from a cabinet of curiosities.

It seems unlikely that Hollar would have embarked on such an ambitious project or labored on it with such evident intensity unless there was the firm prospect of some commercial outlet. The likeliest scenario is that a commission existed from a print or book publisher and that negotiations failed or that funding was not forthcoming. In any event, the unfortunate Hollar seems to have lost possession of the plates.

Shells often formed a part of still lifes by contemporary Netherlandish artists, who could find examples in such ports as Amsterdam and Antwerp. Because of their petrified fragility they were often seen as Vanitas emblems, suggesting the transience and futility of life, but they do not have that connotation in Hollar's prints. Shells formed a part of the cabinet of curiosities of many amateurs, and rare examples were valuable. A portrait in the Ashmolean Museum by Emmanuel de Critz depicts John Tradescant and his friend Zythepsa with the former's collection of shells (see fig. 14).

Rembrandt van Rijn (1606–1669)

The Shell (Conus Marmoreus)

Etching, drypoint, and engraving (White and Boon 159; first state of three)
1650
97 × 132; ¾ × 5¼
Provenance: J. H. Hawkins (L.1471); Earl of Aylesford (L.53); Duke of Buccleuch (L.402); G. W. Vanderbilt (L.15090)

Pierpont Morgan Library, New York; B159i

This is Rembrandt's only etched still life, and it is possible that he was motivated by a desire to emulate Hollar's example. However, Hollar's shells were always excessively scarce and may not have found their way to Holland. It is not impossible that Rembrandt simply was inspired by a shell in his own collection or was influenced by the numerous Dutch still life paintings depicting shells. At one time it was believed that this print was a loose copy of Hollar's *Conus imperialis* (no. 93A), but J. Q. Regteren Altena correctly dismissed this notion.[1] In this early state the background is blank; dense shading is introduced in the second state. Unlike Hollar, Rembrandt gives a shadow to the shell to emphasize its substance. This is one of the rarest and most sought-after of all his prints.

1. "Rembrandt en Wenzel Hollar" in *De kronik . . . van het Rembrandthuis* (Amsterdam, 1959), 81ff.

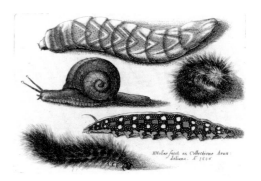

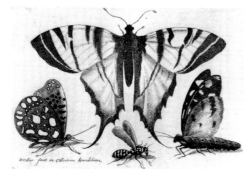
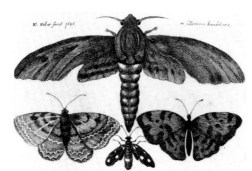

95

Muscarum Scarabeorum, vermiumque Variae Figure & Formae . . .

Etchings (P.2164–P.2175; first state of three)
1646
Each plate: approximately 82 × 119; 3½ × 7½
Provenance: twelve plates from the collection of
Wurtemberg (L. 2606)

Dr. and Mrs. Howard A. Fox

These were etched and published in
Antwerp in 1646 from drawings made in
England. The inscription, "Formae omnes
primo ad vivum coloribus depictae & ex
Collectionae Arundelian," suggests that they
were based on a set of colored drawings or
paintings in the Arundel collection, not on
actual specimens. Indeed, the furry caterpil-
lars in one of the plates could not have been
preserved. However, the design and dis-
placement of the various moths and butterflies seem characteristic of Hollar, and
the series may be a medley of observations
made from life and copies from existing
drawings.

Such natural curiosities formed part of
the cabinets of many collectors. Numerous
small pictures of such exotic assemblages are
known by Jan van Kessel, but he was not
born until 1627 and is thus unlikely to have
been Hollar's source. More likely influences
are the drawings of Georg Hoefnagel and
the engravings of his son Jacob (no. 97),
which Hollar could have seen in Prague and
elsewhere. As observed by Nicholas Penny,
however, the tradition of depicting such
butterflies and insects is rooted in the mar-
ginalia of late medieval illuminated manuscripts.[1]

These works are etched with the greatest
refinement and delicacy of line, and this set
is of the highest quality. Eight impressions
are on paper with a large phoenix-in-laurel-
wreath watermark, frequently found on
prints published in Antwerp at this time.

1. *Thomas Howard, Earl of Arundel* (Oxford, 1985), cat.
59.

96

Forty-One Insects, Moths and Butterflies

Etching (P.2175a)
337 × 215; 13¼ × 8½

Metropolitan Museum of Art, New York, Harris Brisbane Dick Fund; 23.65.35

Unrecorded by Parthey, this print was correctly attributed to Hollar by Pennington, despite the absence of Hollar's signature. One other impression is known, in the Thomas Fisher collection (University of Toronto). The design is an extremely elegant and sophisticated assemblage of separate groups and individual insects from the *Muscarum Scarabeorum* (no. 95).

Jacob Hoefnagel (1575–c.1630)

Archetypa Studiaque Patris Georgii Hoefnagel

Engravings, the set of four title pages and forty-eight plates (Hollstein 17–64)
1592
150 × 206; 5⅞ × 8⅛

Private collection, Switzerland

This celebrated series was engraved by Jacob Hoefnagel at the age of eighteen from drawings by his father. Its purpose was to give wider circulation to the precious illuminations of his father, which were intended for the cabinets of princely collectors, including the Emperor Rudolf. Hollar may well have been familiar with these from his early days in Prague. They combine naturalism with an emblematic purpose, often suggestive of the transience of earthly existence. Thus in this example a moth flutters above a dead mouse and a chrysalis, and the title "Nasci. Patri. Mori." translates as "I am born. I suffer. I die." Hollar, in such plates as *The Dead Mole* and in the multifarious insects of *Muscarum Scarabeorum,* was clearly influenced by the naturalism and the designs of Hoefnagel, but he had little interest in the emblematic substance of their work.

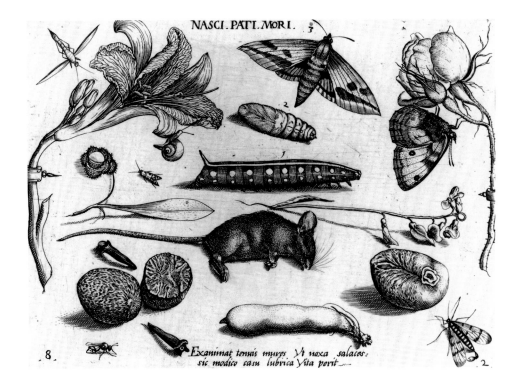

98

A Lady, called Anne Webouts

Etching (P.1728) *far left*
1652
133 × 91; 5½ × 3½

A Lady, called Mary, Countess of Warwick

Etching (P.1729)
1652
133 × 91; 5½ × 3½

Private collection

The sitters were identified in the 1818 catalogue of the Hollar collection of John Towneley, but the identities are unsupported, though both etchings give every appearance of being portraits and not merely fashion studies. These delicately modeled figures, secluded by the heavy curtains behind them, owe much to the miniatures of such English artists as John Hoskins.

99

DAVID DES GRANGES (c. 1611–1675)

Henrietta Maria

Bodycolor on vellum
81 × 69; 3¼ × 2¼

Yale Center for British Art, Paul Mellon Collection; B1974.2.62

This miniature derives from a popular three-quarter-length portrait type of the queen painted by Sir Anthony Van Dyck for Francesco Cardinal Barberini, c. 1636. Des Granges, who is noted for his miniature copies after John Hoskins and Van Dyck, was appointed official limner to Charles II in Scotland.

A

B

C

D

E

F

100

Views Near London

Etchings (P.915–P.919, first state of two; P.920, first state of three)
1665
Each plate: approximately 90 × 127; 3⅜ × 5

Dr. and Mrs. Howard A. Fox

Although unnumbered and without a title, these six etchings clearly constitute a set devoted to the scrubby landscape of Islington, then an outlying district of London. It is a particularly appealing group, with the grand buildings on the skyline contrasted with the rolling curves of earth in the foreground.

A   BY THE WATERHOUSE (P.915)

The Waterhouse was built in 1613, after the construction of the New River, which brought water to London from springs near Ware in Hertfordshire. In this view the spectator is looking southeast.

B   BY ISLINGTON (P.916)

A view taken from the west of the Waterhouse. Old St. Paul's Cathedral is in the distance at the center. The barnlike structure to its left, and nearer the spectator, is the London Spa, which housed a mineral spring and served as a restaurant.

C   BY ISLINGTON (P.917)

The Waterhouse is in the middle distance at the right.

D   ON THE NORTH SIDE OF LONDON (P.918)

A similar view to that in P.916 but drawn from a location farther west. In a hollow in the ground at the center, archers are practicing at the butts.

E   THE WATERHOUSE BY ISLINGTON (P.919)

This view looks east to the Waterhouse.

F   YE WATERHOUSE (P.920)

The spectator is here looking south. Old St. Paul's is behind the Waterhouse at right. A solitary angler is fishing in the foreground. Izaak Walton's *Compleat Angler,* which first appeared in 1653, was so successful that in the author's lifetime it reappeared in new editions in 1655, 1661, 1668, and 1676. Walton, however, sets his anglers in rural situations more idyllic than those depicted by Hollar.

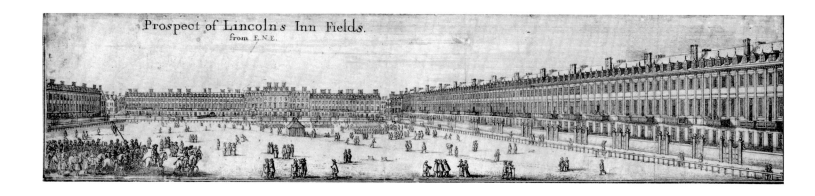

101

Lincoln's Inn Fields

Etching (P.998A)
85 × 389; 3⅜ × 15¼
Provenance: H. Fancourt

British Museum, London

Inscribed "Prospect of Lincoln's Inn Fields from E.N.E," this impression in the British Museum is the only one known. It is unsigned and was obviously never published, but it is clearly by Hollar.

Lincoln's Inn Fields, a large square adjoining Holborn in London, never existed as it is here depicted. The great range of houses on the right was never constructed. Hollar's print probably was etched from a projected design for the square that has now been lost. Hind notes that in about 1641 William Newton was considering the completion of the square and that in 1653 Arthur Newman had purchased the land on the north side with the intention of building on it. The print is undated, but the presence in the square of numerous armed bands, marching and drilling, indicates the period as during the Civil War.

Lincoln's Inn Fields are also depicted (presumably more accurately) in the *Bird's Eye Plan of the West Central District of London.* The ambitious scale and broad perspective of Hollar's print suggest a knowledge of Jacques Callot's *Carrière at Nancy.*[1]

1. Lieure-Meaume 589.

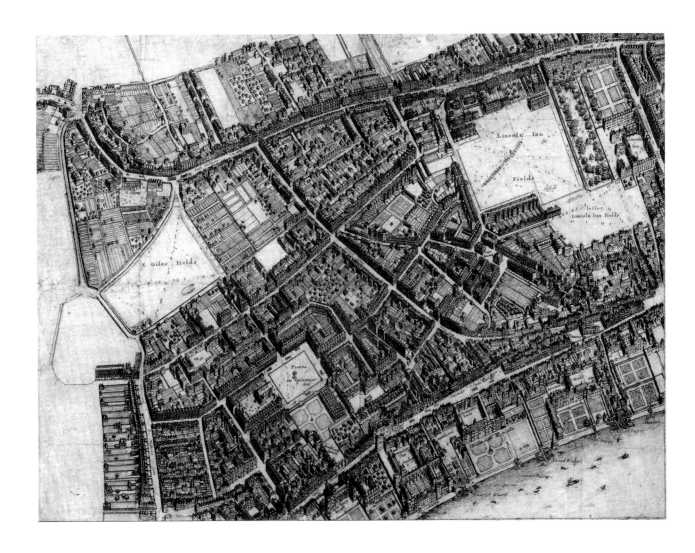

102

Bird's Eye Plan of the West Central District of London

Etching (P.1002)
353 × 457; 13⅞ × 17⅞

British Museum, London

This impression is the only one known to survive from one of Hollar's greatest and most important plates, and it represents the summit of his achievement as a topographer and maker of pictorial maps. It is likely that it was in some way connected with Hollar's work for a Great Map of London, possibly serving as part of a prospectus that he is known to have prepared. Carefully labeled and meticulously drawn, it gives a vivid description of an area of London running from Somerset House by the river to Holborn in the north. The importance of the great spaces of Covent Garden and Lincoln's Inn Fields is particularly evident. A date before the Great Fire of 1666 is evident from its execution. The fire effectively ended Hollar's ambitions of publishing a Great Map, since a view of a London largely vanished had lost much of its commercial potential. The area of London depicted here was untouched by the fire, and the essential layout of many parts of this view is still preserved.

Jupiter, aut ardens evex=
it te Fata vocant: ali-
Vincere, nec duro pote=
Si nunc se nobis ille
Ostendat nemore in

Quos æquus amavit
it ad æthera virtus.
ter non viribus ullis
ris convellere ferro.
aureus arbore ramus
tanto.

ELIÆ ASHMOLE Arm̃o(qui est Mercurio-EX VNO OMNIA philus Anglicus) Tabula merito votiva.

WENCESLAUS HOLLAR AND
WILLIAM FAITHORNE (c.1616–1691)

Aeneas and the Golden Bough

Engraving and etching (P.311; as by Faithorne,
Fagan p. 74)
307 × 197; 12⅛ × 7⅞

Frank W. Raysor II

This is engraved after a drawing by Francis Clein for John Ogilby's *Works of Publius Virgilius Maro. Translated, adorn'd with Sculpture, and illustrated with Annotations,* published in 1654. The figure of Aeneas is evidently engraved by William Faithorne in his most dazzling manner. The landscape has the freer quality of etching, and it is typical of Hollar. The main source of details on Faithorne's life is a short manuscript biography by Thomas Bagford communicated to George Vertue, according to which Faithorne "settled in a house without Temple Bar, at the sign of the Drake, against the Palsgrave's Head Tavern. In this house he continued for several years, and there it was Mr. Wenceslaus Hollar worked and did several plates." There is no other evidence for this, however, and it need be noted that some of Bagford's assertions are demonstrably false (such as his statement that Hollar was at the siege of Basing House in the Civil War).

Castrum Royale Londinense   vulgo   the TOWER.

104

The Tower of London

Etching (P.908)
146 × 257; 5¾ × 10⅛

Dr. and Mrs. Howard A. Fox

This is from a set of four undated London views first recorded in a Peter Stent print catalogue of 1662 but probably executed earlier. The White Tower is seen from across the river, with the traitor's gate in front. Hollar uses the masts of the vessels at the right to vary the symmetry of the design.

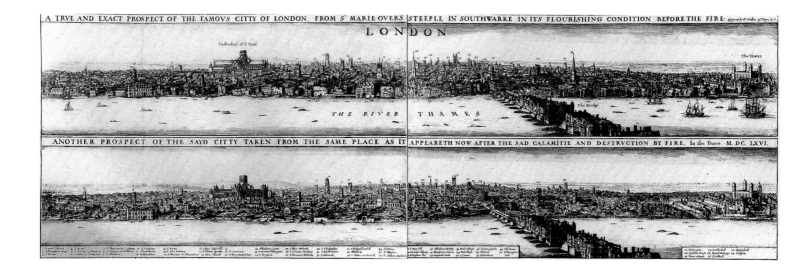

105

London Before and After the Great Fire

Etching (P.1015; first state of five, printed from two plates)
1666
460 × 690; 18 × 27¼

British Museum, London

In five days—from 2 September until 6 September—fire raged in the city of London, reducing five-sixths of it to smoldering rubble. By virtue of his earlier studies of London from bankside Hollar was an ideal candidate to record its depredations, comparing the "Flourishing Condition" of prefire London with the utter desolation that followed. The gutted carcasses of the eighty-nine churches that perished were separated by a wasteland in which only the stone chimneypieces of the old wooden houses survived.

Hollar shows the entire extent of the burned-out area, dominated by the intact Tower of London at the right and the tottering ruin of Old St. Paul's Cathedral at the left. Plans for rebuilding the city were immediately put in hand, and this print would also have served as a tool for Wren, Hooke, or Evelyn, who were preoccupied with ideas—largely frustrated—for building a new and grander metropolis.

106

St. Paul's Cathedral, West Front

Etching (P.1020)
228 × 270; 9 × 10⅝

Yale Center for British Art; DA687 +D8 1858

Hollar's etchings for Dugdale's *History of St. Paul's* constitute the main record of old St. Paul's, which was gutted in the Great Fire and gradually demolished to make way for Wren's new building. Inigo Jones's stately Corinthian portico, the principal subject of the present plate, was the last part of the building to be demolished, lingering on until 1687 or 1688.

The vast structure of old St. Paul's was principally of thirteenth- and fourteenth-century construction, and by the reign of James I it had fallen into a dangerous state of repair. The great steeple had been destroyed by fire in 1561. In 1634 Jones began renovations, but his principal contribution was this Corinthian portico at the west front, which was the personal gift of Charles I, and, with Jones's Banqueting House and the Queen's House at Greenwich, one of the few great contemporary classical structures that England could boast. John Evelyn found it "comparable with any in Europe."

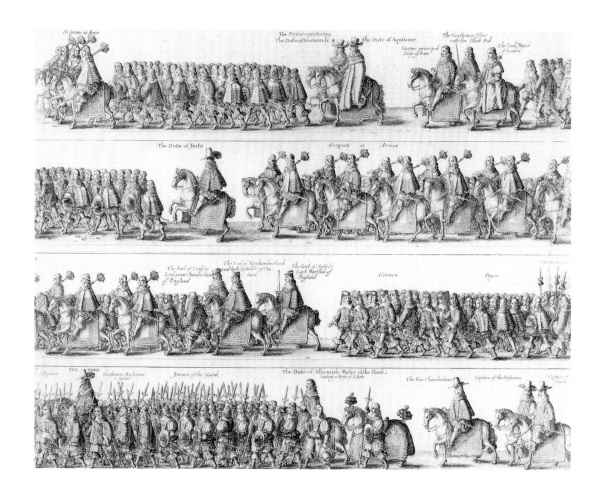

107

The Cavalcade or His Maiestie's Passing Through the City of London Towards His Coronation

Etchings (P.570–P.573)
1662
Each plate: approximately 379 × 492; 14⅞ × 19¼

Yale Center for British Art, Paul Mellon
Collection; B1991.40.111–115

These four prints represent double-page openings in John Ogilby's *The Entertainment of . . . Charles II, in His Passage Through the City of London to His Coronation*. They would form a continuous procession if the horizontal rows were cut and reassembled. The figures are notably lacking in grandeur and gravitas but possess great vivacity.

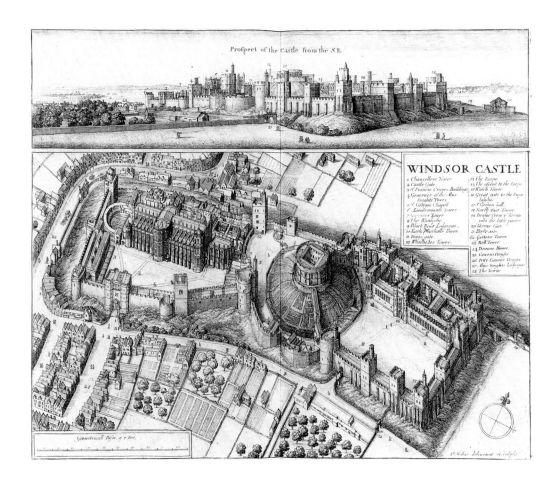

108

A Bird's Eye View of Windsor

Etching (P.1072)
1672
310 × 368; 12¼ × 14⅛

Frank W. Raysor II

This view is from Elias Ashmole's *Order of the Garter*. Ashmole recorded in his diary for 24 May 1659: "I went to Windsor and took Mr. Hollar with me to take views of the castle." Windsor was a favored motif of the artist. This complex aerial view of the castle is among his most sophisticated achievements.

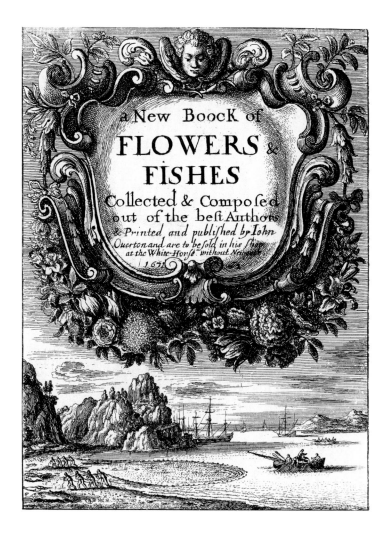

109

Flowers and Fishes

Etching (P.2063; second state of two)
1662
179 × 126; 7 × 5

Robert J. D. Harding

This is the title page to *A New Book of Flowers and Fishes,* published by Peter Stent in 1662 and reissued by John Overton in 1671. The twelve prints contained in the publication are not by Hollar. The delicately etched vignette of fishermen in a bay dragging in their nets was used again by Hollar to illustrate the *Crab and Her Mother* for Ogilby's *Aesopics* (1668).

   This impression is particularly fine and of great interest because it bears the inscription in the lower margin of "Licensed october. 28. 1672 R. L'Estrange." Roger L'Estrange was at this time the Surveyor of the Imprimery, or printing presses. L'Estrange had obtained this position by denouncing offensive and unlicensed publications and pamphlets. Frontispieces to new publications (or in this case reissues) needed his signature before they could be legally issued.

110

John Dunstall (d. 1693)

A Book of Flowers, Fruits, Beasties, Birds and Flies

Etchings
1661
130 × 181; 5⅛ × 7⅛

Yale Center for British Art; QK98 +B61661

Little is known of Dunstall, who died in London in 1693, beyond the fact that he had an establishment in the Strand by the early 1660s and was described by Vertue as "a small professor & teacher of drawing." His sets of etchings of natural history were clearly intended as manuals of instruction and reflect the influence of Hollar at a humble level.

ATTRIBUTED TO WENCESLAUS HOLLAR

The Head and Hind Legs of a Horse's Carcass

Metalpoint (Croft-Murray and Hulton 51)
163 × 154; 6⅜ × 6
Provenance: Vivant-Denon (L.779); Sir Thomas
Lawrence (L.2445); J. P. Heseltine, from whom purchased by the British Museum in 1886

British Museum, London; 1886–5-13–3

Taken from a sketchbook of unknown date,
this sheet relates to three other studies of
dead horses now in the Louvre (Vallardi
Collection, nos. 02401, 02402, and 02404),
and a fourth study formerly in the collection
of the late Paul Oppé.

The rather gruesome subject has no parallel in Hollar's work, since he generally
shied away from disagreeable subjects. Furthermore, the contours and parallel lines of
the shading are rather more prolix and fussy
than is normal for Hollar. As a consequence,
the authorship of the entire group must
remain tentative. Hollar did on occasion use
metalpoint, and the central passage of this
drawing, with its soft curves defining the
collapsed carcass of the beast, has similari-
ties to some of his landscape drawings. If the
drawing is indeed by Hollar, and not by
some contemporary Netherlandish artist, it
adds an entirely new dimension to his work.

ROBERT HOOKE (1635–1702)

Micrographia

A A LOUSE
B A FLEA

Etching and engraving
1665
298 × 191; 11¾ × 7½

Beinecke Rare Book and Manuscript Library,
Yale University

Medical Library, Sterling Hall of Medicine,
Yale University

Robert Hooke was one of the most brilliant
and versatile of Hollar's London contemporaries. As an architect he was closely associated with Wren in the replanning of
London, but he is best remembered as the

architect of Bethlehem Hospital (Bedlam). Hooke had been briefly apprenticed to Sir Peter Lely but quickly left his studio on account of an aversion to the smell of oil paint.

He was also an inventor and an important member of the Royal Society. He perfected the design and use of the microscope, the possibilities of which he showed by the publication of *Micrographia,* with its extraordinary large plates. In an age when many heads were lousy, his choice of subjects to enlarge, such as this head louse, must have been uncomfortable.

Hooke presumably made the drawings for these plates himself, but the engraver, whose work is of high quality, remains anonymous. That profound curiosity about the natural world that is innate to Hollar and to many of his contemporaries is wonderfully embodied in Hooke. His breathless diary (for the years 1672–1680) reveals his energy and diversity, and it is to be regretted that no artist seems to have drawn his portrait. Hooke's diary entry for 8 August 1673 records a visit to Hollar and gives a vivid flavor of Hooke's routine and company: "Received a letter from Bishop of Sarum. at Lord Mayors, heard of Lord Chancellor speaking against me in the Councell. thence to Dr. Lock. to Dr. Wrens. to Mr. Hollar with Ogilby, he gave me Tangier prospect. Dind at Mr. Boyles. denyd Brett. viewd books at Pitts with mr. Weekes about Ald. Jefferys—at Garways. Eat Beans and bacon going to bed. slept but 2 houres."

Dr. Locke and Mr. Boyle are, respectively, the celebrated philosopher and chemist, and both were active members of the Royal Society. In 1673 Overton published the twelve etchings of *Divers prospetcs in and about Tangier. Exactly delineated by W:Hollar.* Hooke visited Hollar a week later on 16 August and noted: "at Mr. Hollar concluded scale of 100 in an inch." This presumably refers to a print on which they were collaborating. Its identity is not known, though it is reasonable to assume that it was an architectural subject.

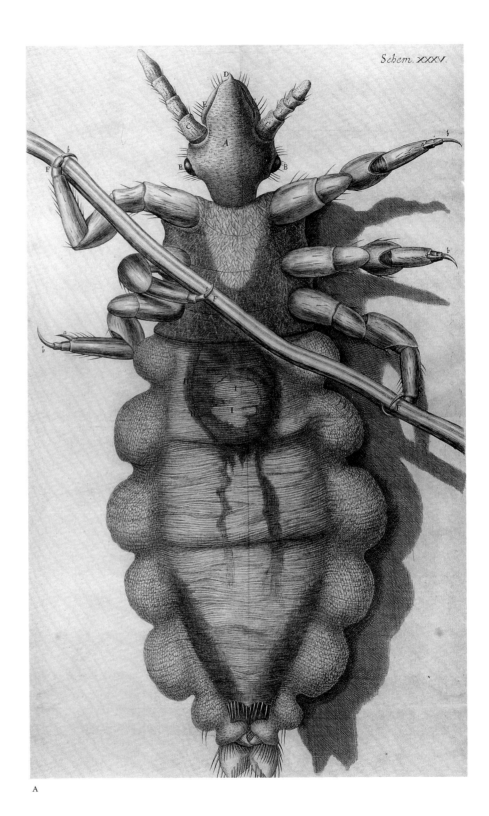

A

FRANCIS BARLOW (1626–1704)

Two Men Examining a Monolith

Graphite, pen and ink with gray washes; verso prepared
in black for transfer to a copper plate
190 × 130; 7 × 5

British Museum, London; 1993–12–11–5

A shepherd and his rustic companion look
with wonder at a megalithic burial chamber
in a sylvan and romantic scene that evokes
the antiquarian enthusiasm of Hollar's
friend John Aubrey, and the wonder Aubrey
felt on discovering Avebury. This design is
unusual for Barlow, who is known primarily
for his paintings and etchings of animals.

Jᴏʜɴ Eᴠᴇʟʏɴ (1620–1706)

Italian Landscape

Pen and brown ink over pencil
1656
Dated and inscribed: 1656, "Titianus invent, J. Evelyn Imitavit"
192 × 302; 7⁹⁄₁₆ × 11⅞

Yale Center for British Art, Paul Mellon Fund;
B1977.7.3

This is based on a celebrated drawing by Titian that is now lost and known only by a number of distinguished copies. Until 1975 Titian's original drawing was believed to be the sheet in the Fondation Custodia (Coll. F. Lugt), Institut Neerlandais, Paris, but it was then identified by Christopher White as a copy by Rembrandt.[1] Titian's original was also copied by Watteau, his drawing, like Rembrandt's, showing in the foreground a bear devouring a goat. A third copy, in the

Louvre, is tentatively attributed to the school of Carracci. This copy omits the incident of the bear and the goat, and is likely to have been the sheet that Evelyn copied. It should be observed that in drawing the naked figure on the right Titian appears to have been recalling Michelangelo's famous Cascina cartoon. It is a measure of Evelyn's sophistication as a connoisseur that his name as a copyist should appear in such august company.

Evelyn was an enthusiastic amateur artist and a pioneer of etching in England, besides being an extremely important connoisseur and promoter of the arts. His book *Sculptura* is the first history of prints to be written in any language, and it introduced the

new art of mezzotint to the English public. He was a friend of Hollar and collected his prints, lamenting the fact that his collection was incomplete. He also commissioned an engraved portrait of himself from Nanteuil when he was in Paris, where he also bought prints directly from the Florentine etcher Della Bella. Evelyn is one of the greatest and most sympathetic Englishman of his time. He was deeply concerned with such issues as the pollution of London, the rebuilding of the city after the Great Fire, and the founding of the Royal Society, though he is best remembered today for his informative diaries.

1. *Master Drawings*, XIII, 375–379.

PRINCE RUPERT (1619–1682)
The Standard Bearer

Mezzotint, after Pietro della Vecchia (first state of
three; Chaloner-Smith 5, Hind 4)
278 × 197; 10⅞ × 7¾

Yale Center for British Art, Paul Mellon
Collection; B1970.3.19

Prince Rupert was the nephew of Charles I
and celebrated as a flamboyant commander
of cavalry in the Civil War. He also commanded a flotilla of royalist ships before
spending the rest of the Interregnum in
exile in Cassel, Frankfurt, and Brussels. It
was in Frankfurt that he began experiment-
ing with mezzotint, a technique that had
been pioneered in 1642 by Ludwig van
Siegen's portrait of *Amelia Elizabeth*. In 1657
Prince Rupert arrived in Frankfurt, and in
collaboration with the Dutch artist Waller-
ant Vaillant produced a series of beautiful
mezzotints frequently copied from paintings
by Ribera or artists of the Venetian school.

   His principal contribution to the art lay
in the development of the rocker, a multi-
toothed instrument that with frequent
application covered a copper plate with
myriad tiny indentations. Thus prepared,
the plate would print as a solid mass of
black. The engraver then used a scraper to
modulate those areas that were to show as
tones of white. The method thus proceeded
from black to white, a reversal of orthodox
etching and engraving methods.

   In 1661 Rupert revealed his method to
John Evelyn in England, and the latter published it, together with Rupert's mezzotint
Small Head of an Executioner, in his book
Sculptura (1662). This was the foundation of
the popularity of the technique in England.
Technically conservative, Hollar never attempted the medium, but its popularity
must have contributed to the eclipse of his
own success.

   The original design for this mezzotint was
wrongly attributed by Prince Rupert to
Giorgione, to whom many Venetian works
of a poetic nature were incorrectly given.

English Views

A HASCOMB HILL IN SURREY (P.950)
B THE RUINS OF BRAMBER CASTLE IN
   SUSSEX (P.951)
C ISLE OF WIGHT (P.952)

Etchings (P.950, first state of two; P.951, second state of
two; P.952, only state)
Each plate: approximately 85 × 136; 3⅜ × 5⅜
Provenance: P.950: Colonel G. A. Cardew (L.1134)

Dr. and Mrs. Howard A. Fox

These three prints are from a group of five
English rural views that were seemingly
never issued as a set by the artist. They are
neither signed nor dated, but the attribution
is certain.

The placid curves of the hills in southern
England were greatly to Hollar's taste, and
the formalized curves of ground, running
gently from left to right, is entirely characteristic. There is a greater sense of energy in
the *Isle of Wight,* in which two riders gallop
toward the city of Portsmouth, where a
number of naval vessels are riding at
anchor.

A

B

C

117

FRANCIS PLACE (1647–1728)

View up River Showing the City Churches

Graphite with pen and ink; tabs of paper with
additional drawing attached at upper left
125 × 320; 5 × 12⅝

Victoria and Albert Museum, London; E1512/1931

Francis Place is the most interesting English artist to be associated with Hollar, and the nearest approach to a direct follower. Born of genteel Yorkshire stock, he was sent to London when he was seventeen or eighteen, and he entered Gray's Inn to study law. Law had little appeal for him, however, and after meeting Hollar he became friendly with the older man, learned how to etch, and later collaborated with him, particularly in the production of small grotesque heads in Leonardo's manner. He also copied Hollar's work, was employed by John Ogilby, and experimented with the new art of mezzotint. After Hollar's death Place became a gentleman of private means, able to indulge his penchant for travel and for drawing landscapes.

In the 1680s Place was particularly involved in York with a group of like-minded men who styled themselves the York Virtuosi and occupied themselves with investigations of art and the natural sciences. They embodied the practical curiosity of an age that had seen the birth of the Royal Society and great leaps forward in human understanding of the natural world. Place is an attractive figure—an amateur, but one whose vitality of touch and observation makes him one of the founders of the English tradition of drawing from nature.

This precise study, taken from a vantage point near Somerset House, shows the Thames, swarming with small craft. The view is up the river to London Bridge, which is visible at the right, with the Tower of London at its left extremity. In the center is the tall column of the Monument, a memorial to the Great Fire that was erected between 1672 and 1677 from a design by Wren (who was possibly assisted by Robert Hooke). A *terminus atque quem* for the drawing is the presence at the extreme left of Inigo Jones's Corinthian portico to old St. Paul's Cathedral. The portico was demolished in 1687 and 1688 as work on Wren's structure advanced. This was the last portion of the old building to be demolished, and if, as seems likely, Place made this drawing in 1687, one of its purposes must have been to record the dominating grandeur of this great fragment. Many Londoners must have mourned its passing. To the right of the portico is the beautiful steeple of the church of St. Mary-le-Bow, a Wren building completed in 1680. This, like the portico, is drawn onto a separate scrap of paper glued to the sheet. Other newly completed Wren buildings are seen beyond.

118

Francis Place (1647–1728)
Windsor Castle

Graphite with pen and ink and gray wash
189 × 360; 7⁷⁄₁₆ × 14³⁄₁₆

Yale Center for British Art, Paul Mellon
Collection; B1975.3.1227

It is probable that this drawing dates from
the early 1680s. Windsor Castle was a motif
beloved by Hollar, but Place's study is less
factual than the latter's etchings and more
concerned with the disposition of light and
shade to define the mass of the building.

119

Francis Place (1647–1728)

Lambeth from Millbank

Pen and ink with watercolor
c. 1683
95 × 303; 3¾ × 12⅛
Inscribed at lower left: "Lambeth From Millbang besids
my Lord Peterborough's house"
Provenance: By descent from the artist to Patrick Allan
Fraser, Arbroath; Fraser sale, Sotheby's, 10 June 1931

Victoria and Albert Museum, London; E1509/1931

This sheet forms a continuation to Place's drawing of Peterborough House (no. 120) and must be from the same sketchbook. They formed the basis for a finished drawing in the Victoria and Albert Museum of *Peterborough House and Lambeth from Millbank,* which is dated 1683.

Although Place was greatly influenced by Hollar, he was by his own admission never his pupil, and he developed his own method of drawing. Eschewing Hollar's more regular, rolling, and undulating lines, Place used short nervous touches of the pen, and his washes of watercolor are more suggestive of atmosphere. Lambeth Palace, seen across the river was (and is) the residence of the Archbishops of Canterbury and was etched by Hollar. The gentleman with a fishing rod scrambling up the bank vividly evokes Place's enthusiasm for angling. The view is taken from a spot just to the left of the present Tate Gallery.

120

Francis Place (1647–1728)

Peterborough House, London

Pen and ink with watercolor
95 × 303; 3¾ × 11^{15}⁄$_{16}$
Inscribed above the buildings: "Peterborough house: westminster Abbey"
Provenance: By descent from the artist to Patrick Allan Fraser, Arbroath; Fraser sale, Sotheby's, 10 June, 1931

Victoria and Albert Museum, London; E1508/1931

This sheet is continuous with another of Lambeth from Millbank (no. 119) forming Place's most original panoramic view.

Francis Place (1647–1728)

William Lodge

Mezzotint (Chaloner-Smith 7; Hake 210)
156 × 125; 6⅛ × 4⅞

Yale Center for British Art, Paul Mellon
Collection; B1970.3.17

The identification of the thoughtful and
melancholic sitter depends on an old
inscription on the impression in the British
Museum, which also identifies the artist as
Francis Place. Lodge (1649–1689) was a
minor artist and etcher, the translator of
Bari's *Viaggio Pittoresco d'Italia* and a member of the York Virtuosi. Close friends and
keen anglers, Place and Lodge went on a
sketching tour in Wales in 1678.

Place was an early and original exponent
of mezzotint, using his own designs and also
copying the portraits of such artists as John
Greenhill. It was a medium that soon became harnessed to formal portraiture. The
small scale of this print and its intimate per-
ception of the sitter represents a use of the
medium that unfortunately remained unex-
ploited. This print is of the greatest rarity
and was never published. It was presumably
intended for circulation among friends.

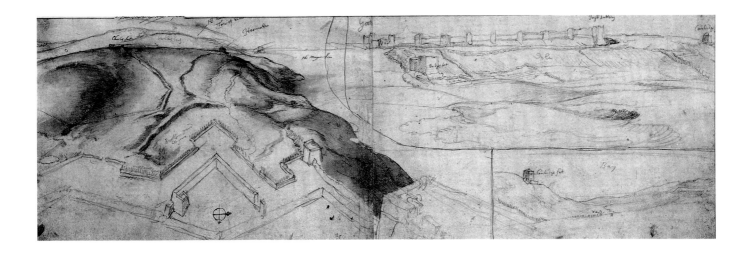

122

View of the Fortifications around Tangier; Southward

Pen and gray ink
203 × 619; 8 × 24⅜

Yale Center for British Art, Paul Mellon
Collection; B1977.14.6205

It is possible that this is a preparatory sketch
for a watercolor that does not
survive.

123

Catherine, Princess of Portugal

Etching (P.1448; first state of two)
1661
217 × 153; 8½ × 6

Metropolitan Museum of Art, New York, Harris Brisbane Dick Fund, 1928; 28.7.7

This is a reduced copy of the same picture used by William Faithorne for his engraving. It is particularly revealing of Hollar's strengths and weaknesses; the face lacks character and form, but the etching of her lace collar is very fine.

124

WILLIAM FAITHORNE (c. 1616–1691)

Catherine of Braganza

Engraving (Fagan p. 9; second state of three)
368 × 273; 14½ × 10¾

Metropolitan Museum of Art, New York, Rogers Fund, 1922; 22.42.3

Catherine was born in 1638, the daughter of John IV, King of Portugal, and married Charles II in 1662. This finely worked engraving bears a royal privilege, indicating a royal favor not granted to Hollar's etched portrait (no. 123).

Faithorne was the preeminent portrait engraver in London during Hollar's lifetime. His early portraits, engraved in a broad manner influenced by Claude Mellan, were mainly published by Robert Peake the Younger. He was a royalist and was taken prisoner at the siege of Basing House in 1645. He spent some time in France, where he was influenced by Nanteuil, before returning to London, where he had a long and successful career. Unlike Hollar he was an able businessman, combining engraving with a print-selling business. For a while, on his return from Antwerp, it is possible that Hollar lodged at his house.

Both Hollar's and Faithorne's prints were based on a painting that was apparently sent to England prior to the royal marriage and was once in Horace Walpole's collection.[1]

1. Strawberry Hill Sale, p. 204, no. 94.

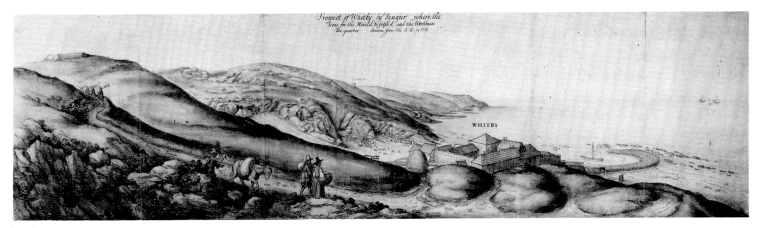

See plate 11

The Settlement at Whitby, West of Tangier

Pen and ink with gray wash and watercolor; on seven conjoined sheets of paper (Croft-Murray and Hulton 32)
280 × 97; 11 × 38½
Provenance: Bequeathed by Sir Hans Sloane to the British Museum in 1753

British Museum, London; 5214–21

This is a view looking northwest from the road to Tangier. The scene is placid, with a couple with a mule descending quietly to the settlement at Whitby. The platoon of musketeers climbing a road at the left remind us, however, that the colony at Tangier was always threatened by hostile forces.

Hollar went to Tangier in 1669 as the King's Scenographer, and the watercolors he made there are his largest and grandest drawings. Tangier came into England's possession as part of the dowry of Catherine of Braganza when she married Charles II in 1662. Another portion of her dowry was the city of Bombay, England's first foothold on the subcontinent. Tangier was abandoned by the English, and its elaborate fortifications were demolished in 1683.

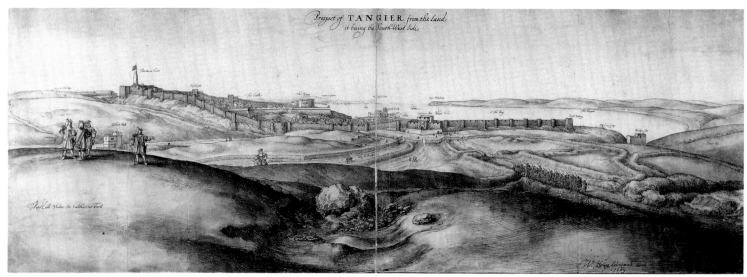

See plate 12

126

Tangier from the South-West

Pen and brown ink, with gray wash and watercolors; on
three conjoined sheets (Croft-Murray and Hulton 28)
323 × 889; 12¾ × 35⅛
Provenance: Bequeathed by Sir Hans Sloane to the
British Museum in 1753

British Museum, London; 5214–19

A group of British officers is on the slope at
the left, one of them pointing toward the
fortified town of Tangier beyond. The bay
can be seen beyond the town, with a distant
view of Gibraltar, which was not yet a
British colony. A flag flies from the most
prominent of the fortifications, Peterborough Tower at the left. The various fortifications and strongholds were mostly named
after British towns. A large group of musketeers marches down a road at the right. The
undulating hills around the town are given
great prominence by Hollar, and it is probable that he exaggerated them in the interests
of creating rhythmic patterns of line.

160

127

View of Prague

Etching (P. 879)
1676
55 × 128; 2¼ × 5
Provenance: H. M. Howard (L.1280 b); Francis Springell

Richard Godfrey; purchased for presentation to the Friends of the National Gallery at Prague

This print is known in only one other impression (Royal Library). It is Hollar's last significant etching, and a highly personal one, as he used a drawing made fifty years before to remind him of his native city, which he had not seen since his brief visit with Arundel's embassy in 1636. The view is remarkably unchanged today, though the bank of earth in the foreground is now a main road. The prospect is taken from across the River Vltava and shows the brittle fortifications of S. Lorenzberg like a spine on the hill. If he had been able to stretch his design a little to the right, we would see the spires of Hradčany Castle. In the foreground at the right a beautifully observed group of riders waters its horses. Bitten with great refinement, this view evidently had deep significance for Hollar, who died the year after its execution.

Bibliography

Borovsky, F. A. *Wenzel Hollar. Nachtrage zu Partheys Katalog*. Prague, 1898.

Clark, Sir Kenneth. *A Catalogue of the Drawings of Leonardo da Vinci . . . at Windsor Castle*. 2 vols. Cambridge, 1935.

Corbett, M., and R. W. Lightbown. *The Comely Frontispiece*. London, 1978.

Corbett, M., and M. Norton. *The Reign of Charles I*. Cambridge, 1964.

Denkstein, V. "The Early Drawings of W. Hollar of 1625–30," *Umeni* 25 (1977): 193–223.

Dostal, Eugen. *Wenceslaus Hollar*. Prague, 1924.

Eerde, Katherine S. van. *Wenceslaus Hollar: Delineator of His Time*. Charlottesville, 1970.

———. *John Ogilby and the Taste of His Times*. London, 1976.

Faithorne, William. *The Art of Graveing and Etching*. London, 1662.

George, Dorothy M. *English Political Caricature. A Study of Opinion and Propaganda*. 2 vols. Oxford, 1959.

Globe, Alexander. *Peter Stent circa 1642–1665. London Printseller. A Catalogue Raisonné of His Engraved Prints and Books with a Historical and Bibliographical Introduction*. Vancouver, 1985.

Grossman, F. G. *Wenceslaus Hollar, 1607–1677: Drawings, Paintings and Etchings*. Manchester, 1963.

Godfrey, Richard T. *Printmaking in Britain: A General History From Its Beginnings to the Present Day*. Oxford, 1978.

———. "Hollar's Last View of Prague." *Print Quarterly* 9 (September 1992): 278–290.

Hake, Henry M. "Some Contemporary Records Relating to Francis Place." *Walpole Society* 9 (1922): 39–69.

Hlavacek, Lubo. "Kosmografie Vaclava Hollara." *Umeni* 15 (1967): 547, 576–580.

Hervey, Mary F. S. *The Life, Correspondence & Collections of Thomas Howard, Earl of Arundel*. Cambridge, 1921.

Hind, Arthur M. *Engraving in England in the Sixteenth and Seventeenth Centuries*. Part 1, *The Tudor Period*. Cambridge, 1952. Part 2, *The Reign of James I*. Cambridge, 1955.

———. "Wenceslaus Hollar." *Print Collector's Quarterly* 17 (1930): 7–22, 117–137.

Hodnett, Edward. *Francis Barlow: First Master of English Book Illustration*. Berkeley, 1978.

Honour, H. "York Virtuosi." *Apollo* 71 (1957): 143–145.

Hooke, Robert. *The Diary of Robert Hooke, 1672–80*. Ed. Henry W. Robinson and Walter Adam. London, 1935.

Howarth, David, et al. *Thomas Howard, Earl of Arundel*. Oxford: Ashmolean Museum, 1985–1986.

Josten, C. H., ed. *Elias Ashmole (1617–1692)*. Oxford, 1966; London, 1988.

Kesnerova, G. "Nova Pragensia Vaclava Holara." *Umeni* 26 (1990): 341–342.

Keynes, Sir Geoffrey. *John Evelyn*. Oxford, 1968.

———. *William Harvey*. Oxford, 1962.

Kratchovil, Milos. *Hollar's Journey on the Rhine*. Prague, 1965.

Layard, George S. *Catalogue of Engraved British Portraits from Altered Plates*. Arranged by H. M. Latham, 1927.

Levis, Howard C. *A Descriptive Bibliography of the Most Important Books . . . Relating to the Art and History of Engraving and the Collecting of Prints*. London, 1912.

Maddison, Francis. *Sir William Dugdale*. Warwick, 1953.

Martin, Margery. "Wenceslaus Hollar and the British Antiquaries." *Motif*, 4 March 1960.

Mielke, Hans. *Wenzel Hollar. 1607–1677: Zeichnungen und Radierungen aus Dem Berliner Kupferstichkabinett*. Berlin: Staatliche Museen Preussischer Kulturbesitz, 1984.

Millar, Sir Oliver. *Van Dyck, Wenceslaus Hollar & The Miniature Painters at the Court of the Early Stuarts*. London: Queen's Gallery, Buckingham Palace, 1968.

———. *The Age of Charles I: Painting in England. 1620–1649*. London: Tate Gallery, 1972.

———. *Van Dyck in England*. London: National Portrait Gallery, 1982.

Millar, Sir Oliver, and Margaret Whinney. *English Art, 1625–1714*. Oxford, 1957.

Noon, Patrick. *English Portrait Drawings and Miniatures*. New Haven: Yale Center for British Art, 1979.

O'Donaghue, Freeman Marius. *Catalogue of Engraved British Portraits . . . in the British Museum*. 6 vols. London, 1908–1925.

Paris Institut Neelandais. *Wenzel Hollar 1607–1677*. Paris, 1979.

Parry, Graham. *Hollar's England, A Mid Seventeenth-Century View*. Salisbury, 1980.

Pauli, Gustav. "Verschollene Durer-Zeichnungen in Radierungen W. Hollars." In *Jahrbuch fur Kunstsammler*, vol. 1. Frankfurt, 1921.

Pav, J. I. "Wenceslaus Hollar in Germany 1627–36." *Art Bulletin* 55 (January 1973).

Pitman, M. C. "Henry Peacham." Thesis, University of London, 1934.

Springell, Francis C. "Unpublished Drawings of Tangier by W. Hollar." *Burlington Magazine* 106 (1964): 69.

Stephens, F. G., and Dorothy George. *Catalog of Political and Personal Satires*. 6 vols. London: British Museum, 1870.

Tyler, Richard. *Francis Place, 1647–1728: An Exhibition Representing All Aspects of His Work*. York: York City Art Gallery, 1971.

Urzidil, Johannes. *Hollar: A Czech Emigré in England*. London, 1942.

Vickers, Michael. "Hollar and the Arundel Marbles." *Country Life*, 29 March 1979.

Index